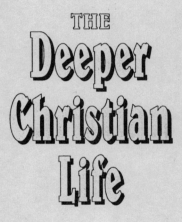

THE

# Deeper
# Christian
# Life

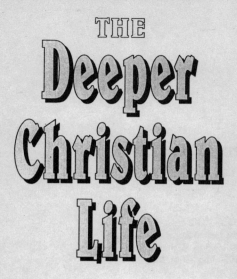

# THE
# Deeper
# Christian
# Life

*Andrew Murray*

w *Whitaker House*

# THE DEEPER CHRISTIAN LIFE

ISBN: 0-88368-298-2
Printed in the United States of America
Copyright © 1995 by Whitaker House
Images © 1994 PhotoDisc, Inc.

Whitaker House
580 Pittsburgh Street
Springdale, PA 15144

2  3  4  5  6  7  8  9  10  11 / 05  04  03  02  01  00 99  98  97  96

# *Contents*

1. Daily Fellowship with God ........................... 7

2. Privilege and Experience ........................... 13

3. Carnal or Spiritual? ................................ 29

4. Out of and Into ..................................... 43

5. The Blessing Secured ............................... 57

6. The Presence of Christ ............................. 71

7. A Word to Workers .................................. 87

8. Consecration ....................................... 103

# 1

# *Daily Fellowship with God*

*Truly our fellowship is with the Father, and
with his Son Jesus Christ.*
—*1 John 1:3*

The first and chief need of our Christian
life is **fellowship with God**. The divine life within us comes from God and
is entirely dependent upon Him. As every moment I need afresh the air to breathe, and as
the sun every moment sends down afresh its
light, so it is only in direct, living communication with God that my soul can be strong.

The manna of one day was corrupt when
the next day came. I must every day have fresh

grace from heaven, and I obtain it only in
waiting directly upon God Himself. Begin each
day by tarrying before God and letting Him
touch you. **Take time to meet God**.

To this end, let your first act in your de-
votions be stilling yourself before God. In
prayer or worship, everything depends upon
God taking the chief place in your attention. I
must bow quietly before Him in humble faith
and adoration, speaking within my heart: "God
is. God is near. God is love, longing to communicate Himself to me. God, the Almighty
One, who works all in all, is even now waiting
to work in me and make Himself known."
**Take time until you know God is very
near.**

When you have given God His place of
honor, glory, and power, take your place of
deepest lowliness and seek to be filled with the
spirit of humility. As a creature, it is your
blessedness to be nothing so that God may be
all in you. As a sinner, you are not worthy to
look up to God. Bow in self-abasement. As a
saint, let God's love overwhelm you, and bow
down lower still. Sink down before Him in
humility, meekness, and patience. Surrender
to His goodness and mercy. He will exalt you.
**Take time to bow very low before God.**

Then, accept and value your place in Christ Jesus. God delights in nothing but His beloved Son, and can be satisfied with nothing else in those who draw near to Him. Enter deep into God's holy presence in the boldness which the blood gives, and in the assurance that in Christ you are well-pleasing to God. In Christ you are within the veil. You have access into the very heart and love of the Father. This is the great object of fellowship with God—that I may have more of God in my life, and that God may see Christ formed in me. **Be silent before God, and let Him bless you.**

This Christ is a living Person. He loves you with a personal love, and He looks every day for the personal response of your love. Look into His face with trust until His love really shines into your heart. Make His heart glad by telling Him that you do love Him. He offers Himself to you as a personal Savior and Keeper from the power of sin. Do not ask, Can I be kept from sinning if I keep close to Him? Instead ask, Can I be kept from sinning if He always keeps close to me? Then you will see at once **how safe it is to trust Him**.

We have not only Christ's life in us as a power, and His presence with us as a person, but we have His likeness to be wrought into us. He is to be formed in us so that His form or figure, His likeness, can be seen in us. Bow before God until you get some sense of the greatness and blessedness of the work to be carried on by Him in you today. Say to God, "Father, here am I for You to work in me as much of Christ's likeness as I am able to receive." Then wait to hear Him say, "My child, I give you as much of Christ as your heart is open to receive." The God who revealed Jesus in the flesh and perfected Him will reveal Him in you and perfect you in Him. **The Father loves the Son and delights to work out Christ's image and likeness in you**. Count upon it that this blessed work will be done in you as you wait on God and hold fellowship with Him.

Our likeness to Christ consists chiefly in two things—His death and His resurrection. *"For if we have been planted together in the likeness of his death, we shall be also in the likeness of his resurrection"* (Romans 6:5). The death of Christ was the consummation of His humility and obedience, the entire giving up of His life to God. In Him we are dead to sin. As we sink down in humility and dependence and entire surrender to God, the power of His death works in us, and we are made conformable to His death. Thus, we know Him in the power of His resurrection, in victory over sin, and in all the joy and power of the risen life.

Therefore, every morning, *"yield yourselves unto God as those that are alive from the dead"* (Romans 6:13). **He will maintain the life He gave and bestow the grace to live as risen ones**.

All this can only be in the power of the Holy Spirit, who dwells in you. Count upon Him to glorify Christ in you. Count upon Christ to increase in you the inflowing of His Spirit. As you wait before God to realize His presence, remember that the Spirit is in you to reveal the things of God. Seek in God's presence to have the anointing of the Spirit of Christ so truly that your whole life may every moment be spiritual.

As you meditate on this wondrous salvation, as you seek full fellowship with the great and holy God, and as you wait on Him to reveal Christ in you, you will feel how necessary the giving up of all is to receive Him. Seek grace to know what it means to live as wholly for God as Christ did. **Only the Holy Spirit Himself can teach you what an entire yielding of the whole life to God can mean**. Wait on God to show you in this what you do not know. Let every approach to God and every request for fellowship with Him be accompanied by a new, very definite, and entire surrender to Him to work in you.

*"By faith"* must here, as through all Scripture and all the spiritual life, be the keynote. As you tarry before God, let it be in a deep quiet faith in Him, the Invisible One, who is so near, so holy, so mighty, so loving. Let it also be in a deep, restful faith that all the blessings and powers of the heavenly life are around you and in you. **Just yield yourself in the faith of a perfect trust to the blessed Holy Trinity to work out all of God's purpose in you**. Begin each day thus in fellowship with God, and God will be all in all to you.

# 2

## *Privilege and Experience*

*And he said unto him, Son, thou art ever with me, and all that I have is thine.*
*—Luke 15:31*

The words of the text are familiar to us all. The elder son had complained and said that though his father had made a feast and had killed the fatted calf for the prodigal son, he had never given him even a kid that he might make merry with his friends. The answer of the father was, "*Son, thou art ever with me, and all that I have is thine.*" One cannot have a more wonderful revelation of

the heart of our Father in heaven than this
points out to us. We often speak of the wonderful revelation of the father's heart in his wel-
come to the prodigal son and in what he did for
him, but here we have a far more wonderful
revelation of the father's love in what He says
to the elder son.

If we are to experience a deepening of
spiritual life, we want to discover clearly what
is the spiritual life that God would have us
live; to ask whether we are living that life; and,
if not, to ask what hinders us living it out fully,
This subject naturally divides itself into these
parts:

- The high privilege of every child of
  God.
- The low experience of too many of us
  believers.
- The cause of the discrepancy.
- The way to the restoration of the
  privilege.

## The High Privilege of God's Children

We have here two things describing the
privilege: first, *"Son, thou art ever with me"*—
unbroken fellowship with your Father is your

portion; and secondly, *"All that I have is thine"* —all that God can bestow upon His children is theirs.

God whispers to His children, *"'Thou art ever with me.'* I am always near you. You can dwell every hour of your life in My presence, and all I have is for you. I am a father with a loving father's heart. I will withhold no good thing from you."

In these promises, we have the rich privileges of God's heritage. We have, in the first place, **unbroken fellowship with Him**. A father never sends his child away without the thought that he cares about his child knowing that he loves him. The father longs to have his child believe that he has the light of his father's countenance upon him all day, and that if he sends the child away to school or anywhere that necessity compels, it is with a sense of sacrifice of parental feelings. If it is so with an earthly father, how do you think it is with God? Does He not want every child of His to know that he is constantly living in the light of His countenance? This is the meaning of that word, *"Son, thou art ever with me."*

That was the privilege of God's people in Old Testament times. We are told that *"Enoch walked with God"* (Genesis 5:24). God's promise to Jacob was, *"Behold, I am with thee, and will keep thee in all places whither thou goest, and will bring thee again into this land; for I will not leave thee until I have done that which I have spoken to thee of"* (Genesis 28:15).

God's promise to Israel through Moses was, *"My presence shall go with thee, and I will give thee rest"* (Exodus 33:14). And in Moses' response to the promise, he says, *"For wherein shall it be known here that I and Thy people have found grace in Thy sight? Is it not that Thou goest with us? So shall we be separated, I and Thy people, from all the people that are upon the face of the earth"* (Exodus 33:16). The presence of God with Israel was the mark of their separation from other people. This is the truth taught in all the Old Testament. Since that is so, how much more may we look for it in the New Testament? Thus, to those who love Him and who keep His word, we find our Savior promising that the Father also will love them, and Father and Son will come and make Their abode with them.

Let this thought into your hearts: **the child of God is called to this blessed privilege—to live every moment of his life in fellowship with God**. He is called to enjoy the full light of His countenance. There are many Christians—I suppose the majority of Christians—who seem to regard the whole of the Spirit's work as confined to conviction and conversion, not that He came to dwell in our hearts and there reveal God to us. However, He came not to dwell near us, but in us, so that we might be filled with His indwelling presence.

We are commanded to *"be filled with the Spirit"* (Ephesians 5:18). Then the Holy Spirit would make God's presence manifest to us. That is the whole teaching of the epistle to the Hebrews: the veil has been rent in two. We have access into the holiest of all by the blood of Jesus. We can now come into the very presence of God, so that we can live throughout the day with that presence resting upon us. That presence is with us wherever we. In all kinds of trouble, we have undisturbed repose and peace. *"Son, thou art ever with me."*

There are some people who seem to think that God, by some unintelligible sovereignty, withdraws His face. But I know that God loves His people too much to withhold His fellowship from them for any such reason. The true reason of the absence of God from us is rather to be found in our sin and unbelief, than in any supposed sovereignty of His. **If the child of God is walking in faith and obedience, the divine presence will be enjoyed in unbroken continuity.**

Then there is the next blessed privilege; *"All that I have is thine."* Thank God, He has given us His own Son, and in giving Him, He has given us all things that are in Him. He has given us Christ's life, His love, His Spirit, His glory. *"All things are yours; and ye are Christ's; and Christ is God's"* (1 Corinthians 3:22-23). All the riches of His Son, the everlasting King, God bestows upon every one of His children. *"Son, thou art ever with me; and all that I have is thine."* Is not that the meaning of all those wonderful promises given in connection with prayer: *"Whatsoever ye shall ask in My name, that will I do"* (John 14:13)? Yes, there it is. That is the life of the children of God, as He Himself has pictured it for us.

## The Low Experience of Many of Us

In contrast with this high privilege of believers, let's look at the low experience of many of us. The elder son has been living with his father and serving him *"these many years"* (Luke 15:29). He complained that his father never gave him a kid, while he gave his prodigal brother the fatted calf. Why was this? Simply because he did not ask for it. He did not believe that he would get it, and therefore never asked for it and never enjoyed it. Thus, he continued to live in constant murmuring and dissatisfaction.

The keynote of all this wretched life is evidenced in what the elder son said. His father gave him everything, yet he never enjoyed it. Then he threw the whole blame on his loving and kind father. O beloved, is not that the life of many a believer? Do not many speak and act in this way? Every believer has the promise of unbroken fellowship with God, but he says, "I have not enjoyed it. I have tried hard and done my best. I have prayed for the blessing, but I suppose God does not see fit to grant it." But why not? One says that it is the sovereignty of God withholding the blessing. The father did not withhold his gifts from the older brother in sovereignty. Neither does our Heavenly Father withhold any good thing from them that love Him and walk uprightly (see Psalm 84:11). He does not make any such differences among His children in the way He deals with them. *"God is able to make all grace abound towards you"* (2 Corinthians 9:8) was a promise equally made to all in the Corinthian church.

Some think these rich blessings are not for them, but for those who have more time to devote to religious activity and prayer. Some believe their circumstances are so difficult or so peculiar that we can have no conception of their various hindrances. But do these not think that God, if He places them in these circumstances, cannot make His grace abound accordingly? They admit He could, if He would, work a miracle for them, but they can hardly expect that He would.

In some way, they, like the elder son, throw the blame on God. Thus many are saying, when asked if they are enjoying unbroken fellowship with God: "Alas, no! I have not been able to attain to such a height. It is too high for me. I know of some who have it, and I have read of it, but God has not given it to me for some reason." But why not? You think, perhaps, that you do not have the same capacity for spiritual blessing that others have. The Bible speaks of a joy that is *"unspeakable and full of glory"* (1 Peter 1:8) as the fruit of believing, and of *"the love of God [which] is shed abroad in our hearts by the Holy Ghost which is given unto us"* (Romans 5:5).

Do we enjoy these blessings? If not, why? We desire the blessing, do we? Why not get it? Have we asked for it? We think we are not worthy of the blessing—we are not good enough, and therefore God has not given it. There are more among us than we know of, or are willing to admit, who throw the blame of our darkness and of our wanderings on God! Take care!

And again, what about that other promise? The Father says, *"All that I have is thine."* Are you rejoicing in the treasures of Christ? Are you conscious of having an abundant supply for all your spiritual needs every day? God has all these for you in abundance. *"Thou never gave me a kid!"* (Luke 15:29). The answer is, *"All that I have is thine.* I gave it to you in Christ."

Dear reader, we have such wrong thoughts of God. What is God like? I know no image more beautiful and instructive than that of the sun. The sun is never weary of shining, of pouring out its beneficent rays upon both the good and the evil. You might close up the windows with blinds or bricks, but the sun would shine upon them all the same. Though we might sit in utter darkness, the shining would be just the same. God's sun shines on every leaf, on every flower, on every blade of grass, on everything that springs out of the ground. All receive this wealth of sunshine until they grow to perfection and bear fruit.

Would He who made that sun be less willing to pour out His love and life into me? The sun—what beauty it creates! And my God—would He not delight more in creating beauty and fruitfulness in me, such as He has promised to give? Yet some say, when asked why they do not live in unbroken communion with God, "God does not give it to me. I do not know why, but that is the only reason I can give you—He has not given it to me."

Remember the parable of the one who said, *"I know thou art an hard master, reaping where thou hast not sown and gathering where thou hast not strewed"* (Matthew 25:24). He was accusing his master of asking and demanding what had not given. Oh, let us come and ask why it is that believers live lives of such low experience.

## The Cause of the Discrepancy between God's Gifts and Our Low Experience

The believer is complaining that God has never given him a kid; or, that God has given him some blessings, but has never given the full blessing. He has never filled him with His Spirit. "I never," he says, "had my heart, as a fountain, giving forth the rivers of living waters as promised in John 7:38." What is the cause?

The elder son thought he was serving his father faithfully for *"these many years"* in his father's house, but it was in the spirit of bondage and not in the spirit of a child. His unbelief blinded him to the conception of a father's love and kindness, and he was unable all the time to see that his father was ready, not only to give him a kid, but a hundred or a thousand kids, if he would have them. He was simply living in unbelief, in ignorance, in blindness, robbing himself of the privileges that the father had for him.

So, if there is a discrepancy between our life and the fulfillment and enjoyment of all God's promises, the fault is ours. **If our experience is not what God wants it to be, it is because of our unbelief in the love of God, in the power of God, and in the reality of God's promises**.

In the story of the Israelites, God's word teaches us that it was unbelief on their part that was the cause of their troubles, and not any limitation or restriction on God's part. As Asaph said in Psalm 78: *"He clave the rocks in the wilderness, and gave them drink as out of the great depths. He brought streams also out of the rock, and caused waters to run down like rivers"* (vv. 15-16). Yet they sinned by doubting His power to provide meat for them: *"They spake against God; they said, can God furnish a table in the wilderness?"* (v. 19). Later on, we read, *"They turned back and tempted God, and limited the Holy One of Israel"* (v. 41). They kept distrusting Him from time to time. When they got to Kadesh-Barnea, and God told them to enter the land flowing with milk and honey where would be rest, abundance, and victory, only two men said, "Yes, we can take possession, for God can make us conquer." But the ten spies and the six hundred thousand men answered, "No, we can never take the land; the enemies are too strong for us." It was simply unbelief that kept them out of the land of promise.

**If there is to be any deepening of the spiritual life in us, we must come to the discovery and the acknowledgment of the unbelief that is in our hearts**. God grant that we may get this spiritual quickening, and that we may come to see that it is by our unbelief that we have prevented God from doing His work in us.

**Unbelief is the mother of disobedience, and of all sins and shortcomings**— temper, pride, unlovingness, worldliness, sins of every kind. Though these differ in nature and form, yet they all come from the one root, namely, that we do not believe in the freedom and fullness of the divine gift of the Holy Spirit to dwell in us and strengthen us, and fill us with the life and grace of God all the day long. Look, I pray you, at that elder son, and ask what was the cause of that terrible difference between the heart of the father and the experience of the son. There can be no answer but that it was this sinful unbelief that utterly blinded the son to a sense of his father's love.

Dear fellow believer, I want to say to you that if you are not living in the joy of God's salvation, the entire cause is your unbelief. You do not believe in the mighty power of God, and that He is willing by His Holy Spirit to work a thorough change in your life and enable you to live in fullness of consecration to Him. God is willing that you should so live, but you do not believe it. **If men really believed in the infinite love of God, what a change it would bring about!**

What is love? It is a desire to communicate oneself for the good of the object loved. It is the opposite of selfishness, as we read in 1 Corinthians 13:5, "[Love] *seeketh not her own.*" Thus, the mother is willing to sacrifice herself for the good of her child. Just so, God in His love is ever willing to impart blessing. He is omnipotent in His love. This is true, my friends. **God is omnipotent in love, and He is doing His utmost to fill every heart** in this house. "But if God is really anxious to do that, and if

He is Almighty, why does He not do it now?"
You must remember that God has given you a
will. By the exercise of that will, you can hin-
der God and remain content, like the elder son,
with the low life of unbelief. Come, now, and
let us **see the cause of the difference between God's high, blessed provision for
His children, and the low, sad experience
of many of us in the unbelief that dis-
trusts and grieves Him**.


## The Way to Restoration

We all know the parable of the prodigal
son, and how many sermons have been
preached about repentance from that parable.
We are told that *"when he came to himself, he
said...I will arise and go to my father, and will
say unto him, Father, I have sinned against
heaven, and before thee"* (Luke 15:17-18). In
preaching, we speak of this as the first step in
a changed life—as conversion, repentance, confession, returning to God. But, as this is the
first step for the prodigal, we must remember
that this is also the step to be taken by God's
erring children—by all the ninety-nine *"who
need no repentance"* (Luke 15:7), or think they
do not.

Those Christians who do not understand how wrong their low religious life is must be taught that this is sin—unbelief—and that it is as necessary that they should be brought to repentance as the prodigal. You have heard a great deal of preaching repentance to the unconverted, but I want to try to preach it to God's children.

We have **a picture of so many of God's children in that elder brother**. What the father told him, to bring about a consideration of the love that He bore him just as he loved the prodigal brother, God tells to us in our contentedness with such a low life: "You must repent and believe that I love you, and *'all that I have is thine.'*" He says, "By your unbelief, you have dishonored me, living for ten, twenty, or thirty years, and never believing what it was to live in the blessedness of My love. You must confess the wrong you have done Me in this, and be broken down in contrition of heart just as truly as the prodigal."

There are many children of God who **need to confess** that, though they are His children, **they have never believed that God's promises are true** and that He is willing to fill their hearts all the day long with His blessed presence. Have you believed this? If you have not, all our teaching will be of no profit to you. Will you not say, "By the help of God, I will begin now a life of faith, and will not rest until I know what such a life means. I will believe that I am every moment in the Father's presence, and all that He has is mine"?

May the Lord God work this conviction in the hearts of all cold believers. Have you ever heard the expression, "a conviction for sanctification"? You know that the unconverted man needs conviction before conversion. So does the dark-minded Christian need conviction prior to and in order for sanctification, before he comes to a real insight into spiritual blessedness. He **must be convicted a second time because of his sinful life of doubt, temper, and unlovingness**. He must be broken down under that conviction. Only then there is hope for him.

May the Father of mercy grant to all of His children that deep contrition, so that they may be led into the blessedness of His presence and enjoy the fullness of His power and love!

# 3

## Carnal or Spiritual?

*And Peter went out and wept bitterly.*
*—Luke 22:62*

These words indicate the turning point in the life of Peter—a crisis. There is often a question about the life of holiness: Do you grow steadily into it, or do you come into it suddenly by a crisis? Peter had been growing for three years under the training of Christ, but he had grown terribly downward, for the end of his growing was that he denied Jesus. Then there came a crisis. After the crisis, he was a changed man and was able to begin to grow properly. Indeed, we must grow in grace; but before we can grow in grace, we must be put right.

You know what the two halves of the life of Peter were. In God's Word, we read very often about the difference between the carnal and the spiritual Christian. The word *carnal* comes from the Latin word for flesh. In the eighth chapter of Romans and in the fifth chapter of Galatians, we are taught that the flesh and the Spirit of God are the two opposing powers by which we are dominated or ruled. We are also taught that a true believer may allow himself to be ruled by the flesh. That is what Paul writes to the Corinthians. In the first four verses of the third chapter, he says four times to them that they are carnal, not spiritual. Just so, a believer can allow the flesh to have so much power over him that he becomes or remains *"carnal."*

Every object is named according to its most prominent characteristic. If a man is a babe in Christ and has a little of the Holy Spirit and a great deal of the flesh, he is called carnal, for the flesh is his chief mark. If he gives way—as the Corinthians did—to strife, temper, division, and envy, he is a carnal Christian, He is a Christian, but a carnal one. But if he gives himself over entirely to God so that the Holy Spirit can deliver him from the temper, the envy, and the strife by breathing in a heavenly disposition and mortifying the deeds of the body, then God's Word calls him a "*spiritual*" man, a true spiritual Christian.

Now, these two styles are remarkably illustrated in the life of Peter. The text is the crisis turning point at which he begins to pass from one side to the other. The thought that I want to impart to you is this: **the great majority of Christians are not spiritual men, but they may become spiritual men by the grace of God**. I want to come to all of you who are perhaps hungering and longing for the deeper life, and asking what is wrong that you are without it, to point out that what is wrong is just one thing—allowing the flesh to rule in you and trusting in the power of the flesh to make you good. There is a better life, a life in the power of the Holy Spirit.

I want to tell you a three things. The first thing is important: take care of the carnal life and confess if you are in it. The second truth is very blessed: there is a spiritual life, so believe that it is a possibility. But the third truth is the most important: you can by one step get out of the carnal into the spiritual state. May God reveal it to you now through the story of the Apostle Peter!

Look at Peter, first of all, in the carnal state. What are the marks of the carnal state in him? Self-will, self pleasing, self-confidence.

Just remember, when Christ said to the disciples at Caesarea Philippi, "The Son of Man must be crucified," Peter responded, "Lord, that can never be!" Christ had to say to him, *"Get thee behind Me, Satan."* (See Matthew 16:13-23.) Dear reader, what an awful thing for Peter! He could not understand what a suffering Christ was. And Peter was so self-willed and self-confident that he dared to contradict and rebuke Christ. Just think of it!

Then, you remember, how Peter and the other disciples were more than once quarreling as to who was to be the chief—what self-exaltation, self-pleasing! Every one of them wanted the chief seat in the kingdom of God.

Again, remember the last night, when Christ warned Peter that Satan had desired to sift him and that he would deny the Lord. Peter said twice over, "Lord, if they all deny You, I am ready to go to prison and to death." What self-aggrandizement! He was sure that his heart was right. He loved Jesus, but he trusted himself. "I will never deny my Lord."

Don't you see that the whole of Peter's life was carnal confidence in himself? In his carnal pride, in his carnal unlovingness, in the carnal liberty he took in contradicting Jesus, it was all just the life of the flesh. Peter loved Jesus. God had taught him by the Holy Spirit. Christ had said, *"Flesh and blood hath not revealed it unto you, but My Father which is in heaven"* (Matthew 16:17). God had taught Peter that Christ was the Son of God. Even so, with all that, Peter was still under the power of the flesh. That is why Christ said at Gethsemane, *"The spirit indeed is willing, but the flesh is weak"* (Matthew 26:41), meaning, "You are under the power of the flesh; you cannot watch with Me."

Dear reader, what did it all lead to? The flesh led not only to the sins I have mentioned, but finally to the saddest of things, to Peter's actual denial of Jesus. Three times over he told the lie, once with an oath, "I know not the man." He denied his blessed Lord. That is what it comes to with the life of the flesh. That is Simon Peter.

Now, look next at Peter after he became a spiritual man. Christ had taught Peter a great deal. If you count carefully, you will find some seven or eight times that Christ had spoken to the disciples about humility. He had taken a little child and set him in the midst of them. He had said, *"Whosoever exalteth himself shall be abased; and he that humbleth himself shall be exalted"* (Luke 14:11). Jesus had taught that principle several times. At the last supper He had washed their feet. However, all of Christ's instructions were in vain, for they had not taught Peter humility.

Remember that a man who is not spiritual, though he may read his Bible, though he may listen to the most earnest preaching, though he may study God's Word, cannot conquer sin, because he is not living the life of the Holy Spirit. God has so ordered that **man cannot live a righteous Christian life unless he is full of the Holy Ghost**. Do you wonder at what I say? You have been accustomed to thinking that *"full of the Holy Ghost"* (Acts 6:3) is what the apostles had to be on the day of Pentecost; what the martyrs and the ministers had to be; but for every man to be *"full of the Holy Ghost"* is too high? I tell you solemnly, unless you believe that, you will never become thorough-going Christians. I must be full of the Holy Spirit if I am to be a whole-hearted Christian.

Then, note the change that took place in Peter. The Lord Jesus led him to Pentecost, the Holy Spirit came from heaven upon him, and what took place? The old Peter was gone, and he was a new Peter. Just read his first epistle and notice the theme of "through suffering to glory." This was written by the same Peter who had said, "Of course, Lord, you never can suffer or be crucified," and who, to save himself suffering or shame, had denied Christ. Peter became so changed that when he wrote his epistle, the chief thought is the very thought of Christ, "Suffering is the way to glory." Do you not see that the Holy Spirit had changed Peter?

Look at other aspects. Look at Peter, who was so weak that a woman frightened him into denying Christ. But when the Holy Spirit came, he was bold to confess his Lord at any cost, ready to go to prison and death for Christ's sake. The Holy Spirit had changed the man.

Look at his views of divine truth. He could not understand what Christ taught him; he could not take it in. It was impossible before the death of Christ. But on the day of Pentecost, how he was able to expound the word of God as a spiritual man! I tell you, beloved, **when the Holy Ghost comes upon a man,** he becomes a spiritual man, and **instead of denying his Lord, he denies himself**.

In Matthew 16 when Peter had said, *"Be it far from Thee, Lord this* [being crucified] *shall not be unto Thee"* (v. 22), Christ said to him: "Peter, not only will I be crucified, but you will be crucified, too. *'If any man will come after Me, let him deny himself, and take up his cross* [to die upon it], *and follow Me'"* (v. 24). How did Peter obey that command? He went and denied Jesus. **As long as a Christian is under the power of the flesh, he will continually deny Jesus**. You always must do one of the two—you must deny self, or you must deny Jesus. Alas, Peter denied his Lord rather than deny himself. On the other hand, when the Holy Spirit came on him, he could not deny his Lord, but he denied himself and praised God for the privilege of suffering for Christ.

How did the change come about? The text tells us, *"And Peter went out and wept bitterly."* What does that mean? It means this, that the Lord led Peter to come to the end of himself, to see what was in his heart, and with his self-confidence to fall into the very deepest sin that a child of God could be guilty of—publicly, with an oath, denying his Lord Jesus! When Peter stood there in that great sin, the loving Jesus looked at him. That look, full of loving reproach and pity, pierced like an arrow through Peter's heart, and he *"went out and wept bitterly."*

Praise God, that was the end of self for Peter! Praise God, that was the turning point of his life! He went out with a shame that no tongue can express. As out of a dream, he woke up to the terrible reality, "I have helped to crucify the blessed Son of God." No man can fathom what Peter must have gone through that Friday, Saturday, and Sunday morning. But, blessed be God, on that Sunday, Jesus revealed Himself to Peter: we do know not how, but *"He was seen of Cephas"* (1 Corinthians 15:5). Then in the evening, He came to him with the other disciples and breathed peace and the Holy Spirit upon him.

Later on, you know how the Lord asked him, *"Simon, son of Jonas, lovest thou me?"* (John 21:15-17) three times, until Peter was sorrowful and said, *"Lord, Thou knowest all things; Thou knowest that I love Thee"* (v. 17). What was it that brought about the transition from the love of the flesh to the love of the Spirit? I tell you, the beginning was when *"Peter went out and wept bitterly"* with a broken heart, a heart that would give anything to show its love to Jesus. With a heart that had given up all self-confidence, Peter was prepared for the blessing of the Holy Spirit.

Now, you can easily see the application of this story. Are there not many just living the life of Peter, of the self-confident Peter as he was? Many are mourning under the consciousness, "I am so unfaithful to my Lord; I have no power against the flesh; I cannot conquer my temper. I give way, just like Peter, to the fear of man; people can influence me and make me do things I do not want to do, and I have no

power to resist them. Circumstances get the
mastery over me, and I then say and do things
that I am ashamed of"? Surely, there are more
than one, who, in answer to the question, "Are
you living as a man filled with the Spirit, de-
voted to Jesus, following Him, fully giving up
all for Him?" must say with sorrow, "God
knows I am not. Alas, my heart knows it, too."

As you think it, I come and press you with
the question, "Is not your position, your character, and your conduct just like that of Peter?" Like Peter, you love Jesus, like Peter you
know He is the Christ of God, like Peter you
are very zealous in working for Him. Peter had
cast out devils in His name, had preached the
Gospel, and had healed the sick. Like Peter
you have tried to work for Jesus. But, under it
all, isn't there something that comes up continually? Oh, Christian, what is it? "I pray, I
try, and I do long to live a holy life, but the
flesh is too strong, and sin gets the better of
me. Continually I am pleasing self instead of
denying it, and denying Jesus instead of
pleasing Him." Come, all who are willing to
make that confession, and look quietly at the
other life that is possible for you.

Just as the Lord Jesus gave the Holy Spirit
to Peter, He is willing to give the Holy Spirit to
you. Are you willing to receive Him? Are you

willing to give up yourself entirely as an empty, helpless vessel, to receive the power of the Holy Spirit to live, dwell, and work in you every day? Dear believer, God has prepared such a beautiful and blessed life for every one of us, and God as a Father is waiting to see why you will not come to Him and let Him fill you with the Holy Ghost. Are you willing for it? I am sure some are.

There are some who have often cried, "O God, why can't I live that life? Why can't I live every hour in unbroken fellowship with You? Why can't I enjoy what my Father has given me, all the riches of His grace? It is for me He gave it, and why can't I enjoy it?" There are those who ask of me, "Why, can't I abide in Christ every day, every hour, every moment? Why can't I have the light of my Father's love filling my heart all day long, every day? Tell me, servant of God, what can help me?"

I can tell you one thing that will help you. What helped Peter? *"Peter went out and wept bitterly."* **We must come to a conviction of sin; we must come to a real, downright, earnest repentance, or we never can get into the deeper life**. We must stop complaining and confessing, "Yes, my life is not what it should be, and I will try to do better." That won't help you.

What will help you? Just this—go down in despair at the feet of Jesus, and begin with a very real and bitter shame to make confession, "Lord Jesus, have compassion upon me! For these many years I have been a Christian, but there are so many sins from which I have not cleansed myself—temper, pride, jealousy, envy, sharp words, unkind judgments, unforgiving thoughts." One must say, "There is a friend whom I never have forgiven for what he has said." Another must say, "There is an enemy whom I dislike. I cannot say that I can love him." Another must say, "There are things in my business that I would not like brought out into the light of man." Another must say, "I am led captive by the law of sin and death." Oh, Christians, come and make confession with shame and say, "I have been bought with the blood, I have been washed with the blood, but just think of what a life I have been living! I am ashamed of it." Bow before God and ask Him by the Holy Spirit to make you more deeply ashamed and to work in you that divine contrition. I pray you take this step at once.

*"Peter went out and wept bitterly."* That was his salvation. Yes, that was the turning point of his life. Shall we not fall upon our faces before God, make confession, and get down on our knees under the burden of the

terrible load, and say, "I know I am a believer, but I am not living as I should to the glory of my God. I am under the power of the flesh and all of the self-confidence, self-will, and self-pleasing that marks my life."

Dear Christians, do you not long to be brought near to God? Would you not give anything to walk in close fellowship with Jesus every day? Would you not count it a pearl of great price to have the light and love of God shining in you all the day? Oh, come and fall down and make confession of sin. If you will do it, Jesus will come and meet you. He will ask you, *"Lovest thou Me?"* If you say, "Yes, Lord," very quickly He will ask again, *"Lovest thou Me?"* If you say, "Yes, Lord" again, He will ask a third time, *"Lovest thou Me?"* Your heart will be filled with an unutterable sadness and will get still more broken down and bruised by the question. You will say, "Lord, I have not lived as I should, but still I love You, and I give myself to You."

Beloved, may God give us grace now, that, with Peter, we may go out, and, if need be, weep bitterly. If we do not weep bitterly (we are not going to force tears), may we sigh very deeply, bow very humbly, and cry very earnestly, "O God, reveal to me the carnal life in which I have been living. Reveal to me what has been hindering me from having my life full of the Holy Ghost." Shall we not cry, "Lord, break my heart into utter self-despair, and bring me in helplessness to wait for the divine power, for the power of the Holy Ghost, to take possession and to fill me with a new life which I will give all back to Jesus?"

# 4

## Out of and Into

*And He brought us out from thence, that He might bring us in, to give us the land which He sware unto our fathers.*
*—Deuteronomy 6:23*

I have spoken of the crisis that comes in the life of the man who sees that his Christian experience is low and carnal, and who desires to enter into the full life of God. Some Christians do not understand that there should be such a crisis in their lives. They think that they ought to continue to grow and progress from the day of their conversion onward. I have no objections to that, if they have grown as they should have. If their life has been so strong under the power of the Holy Ghost that they have grown as true believers should grow, I certainly have no objection to this.

But I want to deal with those Christians whose life since conversion has been very much a failure, and who feel it to be such because of their not being filled with the Spirit, as is their blessed privilege. I want to say for their encouragement that by taking one step, they can get out of the failure and into the life of rest, victory, and fellowship with God to which the promises of God invite them.

Look at the elder son in the parable. How long would it have taken him to get out of that state of blindness and bondage into the full condition of sonship? By believing in his father's love, he might have gotten out that very hour. If he had been powerfully convicted of his guilt in his unbelief, and if he had confessed like his prodigal brother, *"I have sinned,"* he would have come that very moment into the favor of his loving father and the enjoyment of the son's happiness in his father's home. He would not have been detained by having a great deal to learn and a great deal to do, but in one moment, his whole relationship would have been changed.

Remember, too, what we saw in Peter's case. In one moment, the look of Jesus broke him down, and there came to him the terribly bitter reflection of his sin—his selfish, fleshly confidence. His contrition in response to that reflection laid the foundation for his new and better life with Jesus.

God's Word foreshadows the idea of the Christian's entrance into the new and better life in the history of the people of Israel as they entered into the land of Canaan. In our text, we have these words, "[God] *brought us out from thence* [Egypt], *that He might bring us in* [to Canaan]." There were two steps—one was bringing them out, and the other was bringing them in. So **in the life of the believer, there are ordinarily two steps quite separate from each other: the bringing him out of sin and the world, and the bringing him into a state of complete rest afterward**.

It was the intention of God that Israel should enter the land of Canaan from Kadesh-Barnea, as soon as He had made His covenant with them at Sinai. But they were not ready to enter immediately because of their sin, unbelief, and disobedience. After that, they had to wander for forty years in the wilderness.

Now, look how God led the people. In Egypt, there was a great crisis, where they had first to pass through the Red Sea, which is a type of conversion. When they went into Canaan, there was a second conversion, so to speak, in passing through the Jordan. At our

conversion, we come into liberty, out of the
bondage of Egypt. But, when we fail to use our
liberty through unbelief and disobedience, we
wander in the wilderness for a longer or
shorter period before we enter into the Canaan
of victory, rest, and abundance. Thus God does
for His Israel two things: He brings them out
of Egypt, and He leads them into Canaan.

My purpose, then, is to ask this question of
the believer: Since you know you are converted
and God has brought you out of Egypt, have
you yet come into the land of Canaan? If not,
are you willing for Him to bring you into the
fuller liberty and rest He has provided for His
people? He brought Israel out of Egypt by a
mighty hand; the same mighty hand brought
us out of our land of bondage. With the same
mighty hand, He brought his ancient people
into rest. By that hand, too, He can give us
into our true rest. The same God who par-
doned and regenerated us—He who puts His
love into our hearts—is waiting to perfect His
love in us if we but trust Him. Are there many
hearts saying: "I believe God brought me out
of bondage twenty, thirty, or forty years ago,
but I cannot say that I have ever been brought
into the happy land of rest and victory?"

How glorious was the rest of Canaan after
all the wanderings in the wilderness! So is it

with the Christian who reaches the better promised Canaan of rest. When he comes to leave all his cares with the Lord Jesus—his responsibilities, anxieties, and worry—his only work is to hand over the keeping of his soul into the hand of Jesus every day and hour. And the Lord can keep and give the victory over every enemy. Jesus has undertaken not only to cleanse our sin and bring us to heaven, but also to keep us in our daily life.

I ask again: Are you hungering to get free from sin and its power? Is there anyone longing to get complete victory over his temper, his pride, and all his evil inclinations? Are there hearts longing for the time when no clouds will come between them and their God, longing to walk in the full sunshine of God's loving favor? The very God who brought you out from the Egypt of darkness is also ready and able to bring you into the Canaan of rest.

And now comes the question again: What is the way by which God will bring me to this rest? What is needed on my part if God is really to bring me into the happy land? I give the answer first of all by asking another question: Are you willing to forsake your wanderings in the wilderness? If you say, "We do not want to leave our wanderings, where we have had so many wonderful indications of God's presence with us. We have had so many remarkable proofs of divine care and goodness, like that of the ancient people of God, who had the pillar to guide them, the manna given to them every day for forty years, and Moses and Aaron to lead and advise them. The wilderness is to us, on account of these things, a kind of sacred place, and we are loath to leave it."

If the children of Israel had said anything of this kind to Joshua, he would have said to them (and we all would have said): "Oh, you fools: It is the very God who gave you the pillar of cloud and the other blessings in the wilderness, who tells you now to come into the land flowing with milk and honey." So I can speak to you in the same way: I bring you the message that He who has brought you thus far on your journey, and has given you such blessings thus far, is the God who will bring you into the Canaan of complete victory and rest. The first question, then, that I would ask you is:

## Are You Ready to Leave the Wilderness?

You know that the mark of Israel's life in the wilderness—the cause of all their troubles there—was unbelief. They did not believe that God could take them into the promised land. And then followed many sins and failures—

lusting, idolatry, murmuring, etc. That has, perhaps, been your life, beloved. You do not believe that God will fulfill His word. You do not believe in the possibility of unbroken fellowship and unlimited partnership with Him. On account of that, you became disobedient and did not live like a child doing God's will, because you did not believe that God could give you the victory over sin. Are you willing now to leave that wilderness life?

Sometimes you are, perhaps, enjoying fellowship with God, and sometimes you are separated from Him. Sometimes you have nearness to Him, and at other times great distance from Him. Sometimes you have a willingness to walk closely with Him, but sometimes there is even unwillingness. Are you now going to give up your whole life to Him? Are you going to approach Him and say, "My God, I do not want to do anything that will be displeasing to You. I want You to keep me from all worldliness, from all self-pleasing. I want You, O God, to help me to live like Peter after Pentecost, filled with the Holy Ghost, and not like carnal Peter."

Beloved, are you willing to say this? Are you willing to give up your sins, to walk with God continually, to submit yourself wholly to the will of God, and have no will of your own apart from His will? Are you going to live a perfect life? I hope you are, for I believe in such a life. I may not believe in the sense in which you understand "perfection" as entire freedom from wrong-doing and all inclination to it—for while we live in the flesh, the flesh will lust against the spirit and the spirit against the flesh—but the perfection spoken of in the Old Testament as practiced by some of God's saints, who were said to *"serve* [the Lord] *with a perfect heart"* (1 Chronicles 28:9).

**What is this perfection? A state in which your heart is set on perfect integrity without any reserve and your will is wholly subservient to God's will.** Are you willing for such a perfection, with your whole heart turned away from the world and given to God alone? Or, are you going to say, "No, I do not expect that I will ever give up my self-will"? It is the devil tempting you to think it will be too hard for you.

Just look at the will of God, so full of blessing, of holiness, of love. Will you give up your guilty will for the blessed will of God ? **A man can do so in one moment when he sees that God can change his will for him.** He can say farewell to his will, as Peter did when he *"went out and wept bitterly,"* after which the Holy Spirit filled his soul on Pentecost.

Joshua *"wholly followed the LORD"* (Numbers 32:12). He failed, indeed, before the enemy at Ai, because he trusted too much in human agency and not sufficiently in God. He failed likewise when he made a covenant with the Gibeonites. Still, his spirit and power differed widely from that of the people whose unbelief drove them before their enemies and kept them in the wilderness. Let us be willing to serve the Lord our God wholly, and *"make not provision for the flesh to fulfill the lusts thereof"* (Romans 13:14). Let us believe in the love and power of God to keep us, and put *"no confidence in the flesh"* (Philippians 3:3).

Then comes the second step: believing that such a life in Canaan land is possible. Many will say, "Oh, what I would give to get out of the wilderness life! But I cannot believe that it is possible to live in this constant communion with God. You don't know my difficulties—my business cares and perplexities. I have all sorts of people with whom I must associate. I have gone out in the morning braced by communion with God in prayer, but before nightfall the pressure of business has driven out of my heart all that warmth of love that I had, and the world has made my heart as cold as before."

We must remember again what it was that kept Israel out of Canaan. When Caleb and

Joshua said, "We are able to overcome the enemy," the ten spies and the six hundred thousand answered, "We cannot do it; they are too
strong for us." Take care, dear reader, that we
do not repeat their sin and provoke God as
those unbelievers did. He says it is possible to
bring us into the land of rest and peace. I believe it because He has said so, and because He
will do it if I trust Him. Your temper may be
terrible; your pride may have bound you a
hundred times; your temptations may *"com-
pass* [you] *about like bees"* (Psalm 118:12); but
**there is victory for you if you will but
trust the promises of God**.

The second question I ask you, beloved, is:

## Do You Believe This Life Is Possible?

Look again at Peter. He had failed again
and again, and went from bad to worse until he
came to denying Christ with oaths. But what a
change came over him! Just study the first
epistle of Peter, and you will see that the very
life of Christ had entered into him. He shows
the spirit of true humility, so different from
his former self-confidence, ·glorying in God's
will instead of in his own. He had made a full
surrender to Christ and was trusting entirely
in Him. Therefore, come today and say to God,

"You so changed selfish, proud Peter, and You can change me likewise." Yes, God is able to bring you into Canaan, the land of rest.

Notice the expressions that are found in the first half of the eighth chapter of Romans: *"The law of the spirit of life in Christ Jesus hath made me free from the law of sin and death"* (v. 2), to *"walk after the Spirit"* (v. 4), *"to be spiritually minded"* (v. 6), to be *"in the Spirit"* (v. 9), to have *"the Spirit of God dwell in you"* (v. 9), *"through the Spirit* [to] *mortify the deeds of the body"* (v. 13), to be *"led by the Spirit of God"* (v. 14), to be *"the sons of God"* (v. 14). These are all blessings which come when we bind ourselves wholly to live in the Spirit. If we live after the Spirit, we have the very nature of the Spirit in us. If we live in the Spirit, we will be led by Him every day and every moment. What if you were to open your heart today to be filled with the Holy Spirit? Would He not be able to keep you every moment in the sweet rest of God? Would not His mighty arm give you a complete victory over sin and temptation of every kind, and make you able to live in perpetual fellowship with the Father and with His Son, Jesus Christ? Most certainly!

This, then, is the second step; this is the blessed life God has provided for us. First, God

brought us out of Egypt. Secondly, He brings
us into Canaan.

Then comes, thirdly, the question:

## How Does God Bring Us In?

He does so by leading us in a very definite
act, namely, that of committing ourselves
wholly to Him and entrusting ourselves to Him
that He may bring us into the land of rest and
keep us in. You remember that the Jordan
River at the time of harvest overflowed its
banks. The hundreds of thousands of Israelites
were on the far side of the river from Canaan.
They were told that the next day God would do
wonderful things for them. The trumpet would
sound, and the priests would take up the ark—
the symbol of God's presence—and pass over
before the people. But there lay the swollen
river. If there still were unbelieving children
among the people, they would have said,
"What fools, to attempt to cross now! This is
not the time to attempt fording the river, for it
is now twenty feet deep." But the believing
people gathered together behind the priests
with the ark. They obeyed the command of
Joshua to advance, but they did not know what
God was going to do! As the priests walked
straight into the water, the hearts of some of

the people began to tremble. They asked,
"Where is the rod of Moses?" However, as the
priests walked forward and stepped into the
river, the waters rose up on the upper side into
a high wall and flowed away on the other side.
A clear passage was made for the whole camp.
Now, it was God who did this for the people,
because Joshua and the people believed and
obeyed Him. The same God will do it today, if
we believe and trust Him.

Perhaps I am addressing a soul who is
saying: "I remember how God first brought me
out of the land of bondage. I was in complete
darkness of soul and was deeply troubled. I did
not at first believe that God could take me out,
and that I could become a child of God. But, at
last, God took me and brought me to trust in
Jesus, and He led me out safely." Friend, you
have the same God now who brought you out
of bondage with a mighty hand, and who can
lead you into the place of rest. Look to Him
and say, "O God, make an end of my wilderness life—my sinful and unbelieving life—a life
of grieving You. Bring me today into the land
of victory and rest and blessing!"

Is this the prayer of your hearts, dear
friends? Are you going to give up yourselves to
Him to do this for you? Can you trust Him that
He is able and willing to do it for you? He can

take you through the swollen river this very moment—yes, this very moment!

God can do even more. After Israel had crossed the river, the Captain of the Lord's host had to come to encourage Joshua, promising to take charge of the army and remain with them. **You need the power of God's Spirit to enable you to overcome sin and temptation**. You need to live in His fellowship—in His unbroken fellowship—without which you cannot stand or conquer.

If you are to venture today, say by faith, "My God, I know that Jesus Christ is willing to be the Captain of my salvation and to conquer every enemy for me. He will keep me by faith and by His Holy Spirit. Though it may be dark to me as if the waters would pass over my soul, and though my condition may seem hopeless, I will walk forward, for God is going to bring me in today, and I am going to follow Him. My God, I follow You now into the promised land."

Perhaps some have already entered in, and the angels have seen them while they have been reading these solemn words. Is there anyone still hesitating because the waters of Jordan look threatening and impassable? Come, beloved. Come at once, and doubt not!

# 5

## The Blessing Secured

*Be filled with the spirit.*
*—Ephesians 5:18*

I may have a little air in my lungs, but not enough to keep up a healthy, vigorous life. But everyone seeks to have his lungs well filled with air. The benefit of it will be felt in his blood and through his whole being. Just so, the word of God comes to us, and says; "Christians, do not be content with thinking that you have the Spirit, or have a *little* of the Spirit; but, if you want to have a healthy life, *be **filled** with the Spirit*'." Is that your life? Or are you ready to cry out, "Alas, I do not know what it is to *be filled with the Spirit,*' but it is what I long for." I want to point out to these souls the path to come to this great, precious blessing which is meant for every one of us.

Before I speak further of it, let me just note one misunderstanding which prevails. People often look upon being *"filled with the Spirit"* as something that comes with a mighty stirring of the emotions, a sort of heavenly glory that comes over them, something that they can feel strongly and mightily. But that is not always the case.

I was recently at Niagara Falls. I noticed and was told that the water was unusually low. Suppose the river were doubly full—how would you see that fullness in the Falls? In the increased volume of water pouring over the cataract and its tremendous noise. But go to a lake where the very same fullness is found, and there is perfect quiet and placidity, the rise of the water is gentle and gradual, and you can hardly notice that there is any disturbance as the lake gets full.

And so it may be with the children of God. To some, the Spirit comes with mighty emotion and a blessed awareness, "God has touched me!" To others, the Spirit comes in a gentle filling of the whole being with the presence and the power of God. I do not want to lay down the way in which it is to come to you, but I want you simply to take your place before

God and say, "Father, whatever it may mean, that is what I want." If you come, giving yourself as an empty vessel and trusting God to fill you, God will do His own work.

Now, the simple question arises as to the steps by which we can come to *"be filled with the Spirit."* I will note four steps in the way by which a man can attain this wonderful blessing. He must say these things:

- First, "I **must** have it."
- Secondly, "I **may** have it."
- Then, "I **will** have it."
- Finally, "Thank God, I **shall** have it."

The first word a man must begin to say, is, "I *must* have it." He must feel that this is a command of God, and he cannot live unfilled with the Spirit without disobeying God. It is a command here in this text, *"Be not drunk with wine, but be filled with the Spirit."* Just as much as a man dare not get drunk, if he is a Christian, just as much must a man be filled with the Spirit. God wants it. Oh, that every one might be brought to say, "I must, if I am to please God, I must be filled with the Spirit!"

I fear there is a terrible self-satisfaction among many Christians who are content with their low level of life. They think they have the

Spirit because they are converted, but they know very little of the joy of the Holy Ghost and of His sanctifying power. They know very little of the fellowship of the Spirit linking them to God and to Jesus. They know very little of the power of the Spirit to testify for God. Yet they are content.

One says, "Oh, that is only for prominent Christians." A very dear young niece of mine once said to me, "Uncle Andrew, I cannot try to make myself better than the Christians around me. Wouldn't that be presumptuous?" I replied, "My child, you must not ask what the Christians around you are, but you must be guided by what God says." She has since confessed to me how bitterly ashamed she has become of that expression, and how she went to God to seek His blessing. Friends, do not be content with that half-Christian life that many of you are living, but say, "God wants it. God commands it. I must be filled with the Spirit."

Look not only at God's command, but look at the need of your own soul. You are a parent who wants your children blessed and converted, but you complain that you haven't power to bless them. You say, "My home must be filled with God's Spirit." You complain about your own soul, of times of darkness and leanness. You complain of watchlessness and wandering. A young minister once asked me, "Why is it I have such a delight in study and so little delight in prayer?" My answer was, "Your heart must get filled with love for God and His Son. Then you will delight in prayer." You complain sometimes that you cannot pray. Your prayers are so short. You do not know what to pray. Something drags you back from the closet. It is because you are trying to live the life without being filled with the Spirit.

Think of the needs of the church around you. You are Sunday School teacher who is trying to teach a class of ten or twelve children, not one of them, perhaps, converted. If they go out from under you unconverted, you are trying to do a heavenly work in the power of the flesh. Sunday School teachers, begin to say, "I must be filled with the Spirit of God, or I must give up the charge of these young souls, for I cannot teach them."

Think of the need of the world. If you were to send out missionaries full of the Holy Ghost, what a blessing that would be! Why is it that many missionaries complain about the foreign field, "There I learned how weak and unfit I am"? It is because the churches from which they go are not filled with the Holy Ghost. Someone said to me a few weeks ago, "They talk so much about the volunteer movement and more missionaries, but we want something else. We want missionaries filled with the Holy Ghost." If the church and the mission field are to come around, we must each begin with himself. It must begin with you. Begin with yourself and say, "O God, for Your sake, for Your church's sake, for the sake of the world, help me! I must be filled with the Holy Ghost."

What folly it would be for a man who had lost a lung and a half, and had hardly half of one lung to do the work of both, to expect to be strong, do hard work, and live in any climate! What folly it is for a man to expect to live a full Christian life unless he is full of the Holy Ghost! And what folly for a man who has only got a little drop of the river of the water of life to expect to live and to have power with God and man! Jesus wants us to come and receive the fulfillment of the promise, *"He that believeth in Me...out of his belly shall flow rivers of living water"* (John 7:38). Begin to say, "If I am to live a right life, if I am in every part of my daily life and conduct to glorify my God, I must have the Holy Spirit—I must be filled with the Spirit." Are you going to say that? Talking for months and months won't help. Do submit to God, and as an act of submission say "Lord, I confess it, I must be filled. Help me!" And God will help you.

Then comes the second step: I *may* be filled. The first had reference to duty. This has reference to privilege—I may be filled. Alas! So many have become accustomed to their low state that they do not believe that they may actually be filled.

What right have I to say that you ought to take these words into your mouth? My right is this: **God wants healthy children**. I saw today a six-month-old child, as beautiful and chubby as you could wish a child to be. With what delight the father and the mother looked at him. How glad I was to see a healthy child. Do you think that God in heaven does not care for His children, and that God wants some of His children to live a sickly life? It is lie! God wants every child of His to be a healthy Christian, but you cannot be healthy Christian unless you are filled with God's Spirit.

Beloved, we have grown accustomed to a style of life, and we see good Christians—as we call them—earnest men and women, but full of failings. We think "Well, that is human. That man loses his temper, and that man is not as kind as should be, and that man's word cannot trusted always as ought to be the case, but..." In daily life we look upon Christians and think, "Well, if they very faithful in going to church, in giving to God's cause, in attending prayer meeting, in having family prayers, and in their profession, etc." Of course, thank God for them and say, "We wish there were more."

However, we forget to ask, "What does God want?" Oh, that we might see that this is meant for us and everyone else. Beloved, God has been longing for these past years, while you never thought about it, to fill you with the Holy Ghost. **God longs to give the fullness of the Spirit to every child of His**.

They were poor heathen Ephesians, only lately brought out from heathendom, to whom Paul wrote this letter—people among whom there still was stealing and lying, for they had only just come out from paganism. But Paul said to every one of them, *"Be filled with the Spirit."* God is ready to do it. God wants to do it. Oh, do not listen to the temptation of the devil, "This is only meant for certain people—a Christian who has a great deal of free time to devote to prayer and to seeking after it—a man of a receptive temperament—that is the man to be filled with the Spirit."

Who is there that dares to say, "I cannot be filled with the Spirit." Who will dare to say that? If any of you speak so, it is because you are unwilling to give up sin. Do not think that you cannot be filled with the Spirit because God is not willing to give it to you. Did not the

Lord Jesus promise the Spirit? Is not the Holy
Spirit the best part of His salvation? Do you
think He gives half a salvation to any of His
redeemed ones? Is not His promise for all, *"He
that believeth in me...out of his belly shall flow
rivers of living water"* ? This is more than fullness—this is overflow! And Jesus has promised
this to everyone who believes in Him. Cast
aside your fears your doubts, and your hesita-
tion, and say, "I can be filled with the Spirit; I
may be filled with the Spirit. There is nothing
in heaven or earth or hell, that can prevent it,
because God has promised and is waiting to do
it for me." Are you ready to say, "I *may*, I *can*
be filled with the Spirit, for God has promised
it, and God will give it"?

We come to the third step when a man
says, "I *will* have it! I must have it; I may have
it; I will have it." When someone says, "I will
have it," in ordinary events, you know he does
everything that he can do to get possession.
Very often a man comes and wants to buy
something. He wishes for it, but *wishing* is
not *willing*. I want to buy that horse, and the
owner asks $200 for it, but I don't want to give
more than $180. I wish for it very much, and I
can go and say, "Do give it to me for $180."
The man says, "No, $200." I love the horse. It
is just what I want, but I am not willing to give

him the $200. At last he says, "You must give
me an answer. I can get another purchaser."
Finally, I say, "No, I want it very much. I long
for it, but I won't give that price."

Dear friends, are you going to say, "I *will*
have this blessing"? What does that mean? It
means, first of all, that you are going to give up
every sin. You are going to look around into
your life, and if you see anything wrong there,
it means that you are going to confess it to Jesus and say, "Lord, I cast it at Your feet. It
may be rooted in my heart, but I will give it up
to You. I cannot take it out, but Jesus, cleanser
of sin, I give it to You." Let it be temper, pride,
money, lust, or pleasure; let it be the fear of
man; let it be anything—but say to Christ at
once, "I will have this blessing at any cost."

Also, it means not only giving up every sin,
but what is deeper than sin, and more difficult
to get at—it means giving up yourself, with
your will, your pleasure, your honor, all you
have, and saying, "Jesus, I am from this moment going to give myself up, that by Your
Spirit You may take possession of me, and that
You may by Your Spirit turn out whatever is
sinful and take entire command of me." This
looks difficult as long as Satan blinds us and
makes us think it would be too hard a thing to
give up all of that. But if God opens our eyes

for one minute to see what a heavenly blessedness, what riches, and what glory it is to be
filled with the Spirit from the heart of Jesus,
then we will say, "I will give **anything**, but I
will have the blessing." Then, it means that
you are just to cast yourself at His feet and to
say, "Lord, I *will* have the blessing."

Satan often tempts us and says, "Suppose
God were to ask that of you, would you be
willing to give it?" He makes us afraid, but so
many have found that when once they have
said, "Lord, anything and everything!" the
light and joy of heaven filled their hearts.

Last year at Johannesburg, the gold fields
of South Africa, we had testimony time at an
afternoon meeting. A woman rose and told us
how her pastor two months prior had held a
consecration service in a tent. He had spoken
strongly about consecration and had said,
"Now, if God were to send your husband away
to China, or if God were to ask you to go to
America, would you be willing to do it? You
must give yourself up entirely." Her face
beaming with brightness as she spoke, the
woman said that when, at the close of the
meeting, he asked those to rise who were willing to give up all to be filled with the Spirit,
"The struggle was terrible. God might take
away my husband or children from me, and

was I ready for it? Oh, Jesus is very precious,
but I could not say I would give up all. But I
did tell Him I wanted to do it." At last she
stood up. She went home that night in a terrible struggle and could not sleep, for her
thought was, "I said to Jesus *everything*, but
could I give up husband or child?" The struggle
continued till midnight. She said, "But I would
not let go. Finally, I said to Jesus, 'Everything,
but fill me with Yourself.'" Then, the joy of the
Holy Spirit came upon her. Her minister told
me afterwards that her testimony was true,
and for the past two months her life had been
one of exceeding brightness and heavenly joy.

Is any reader tempted to say, "I cannot
give up all"? I take you by the hand, my friend,
and bring you to the crucified Jesus. I say,
"Just look at Him. How He loved you on Cal-
vary! Just look at Him." He offers to fill your
heart with His Holy Spirit, with the Spirit of
His love, His fullness, and His power, actually
to make your heart full of the Holy Spirit. Do
you dare to say, "I am afraid! I cannot do that
for Jesus," or will your heart at His feet cry
out, "Lord, anything, but I must be filled with
Your Spirit"? Haven't you often prayed for the
presence and abiding nearness and love of Jesus to fill you? That cannot be until you are
filled with the Holy Spirit. Cry, in view of any

sacrifice, "I *will* have it, by God's help! Not in my strength, but by God's power, I will!"

Then comes my last point. Say, "I *shall* have it." Praise God that a man dares say that he shall have it. When a man has made up his mind; when a man has been brought to a conviction and sorrow for his sinful life; when, like Peter, he has wept bitterly and sighed deeply before God about the life he has been living; when he has felt wretched with the thought that he is not living the better life, the Spirit life; when a man comes, makes surrender, casts himself upon God, and claims the promise that it is for him, what do you think? Hasn't he a right to say, "I *shall* have it"?

Beloved, I give to every one of you the same message from God, that if you are willing and ready, God is willing and ready to close the bargain at once. Yes, **you can have it now**! Without any outburst of feeling, without any flooding of the heart with light, you may have it. To some it comes in that way, but to many it does not. As a quiet transaction of the surrendered will, you can lift up your heart in faith and say, "O God, here I give myself as an empty vessel to be filled with the Holy Ghost. I give myself up once and forever." With this, the great transaction is done. You can say it now if you will take your place before God.

Ministers of the gospel, have you ever felt the need of being filled with the Holy Ghost? Your heart perhaps tells you that you know nothing of that blessing. Have you ever felt such a need for Christ, "I must be filled with the Holy Ghost"? Children of God, have you ever felt a hope rise within you, "I may have this blessing I hear of from others"? Will you not take the step and say, "I *will* have it"?

Say it not in your own strength, but in self-despair. Never mind if it appears as if the heart is all cold and closed up. Rather, as an act of obedience and of surrender, as an act of the will, cast yourself before Jesus and trust Him. "I shall have it, for I now give up myself into the arms of my Lord Jesus. I shall have it, for it is Jesus' delight to give the Holy Spirit into the heart of everyone. I shall have it, for I do believe in Jesus. He promised me that out of him who believes will flow rivers of living water. I shall have it! I will cling to the feet of Jesus. I will stay at the throne of God. **I shall have it, for God is faithful, and God has promised.**"

# 6

## *The Presence of Christ*

*But straightway Jesus spake unto them saying,
Be of good cheer; it is I; be not afraid.*
*—Matthew 14:27*

All we have had about the work of the blessed Spirit is dependent upon what we think of Jesus, for it is from Christ Jesus that the Spirit comes to us. It is to Christ Jesus that the Spirit always brings us. The one need of the Christian life day by day and hour by hour is this—the presence of the Son of God. God is our salvation. If I have Christ with me and Christ in me, I have full salvation.

We have spoken about the life of failure and the flesh, the life of ups and downs, the life of unbelief and disobedience, the wilderness life of sadness and sorrow. But, we have heard and believed that there is deliverance. Bless God, He brought us out of Egypt so that He might bring us into Canaan, into the very rest of Christ. He is our peace and our rest.

If I may only have the presence of Jesus as the victory over every sin, the presence of Jesus as the strength for every duty, then my life will be in the full sunshine of God's unbroken fellowship. The word will be fulfilled to me in most blessed experience, *"Son, thou art ever with me, and all I have is thine."* My heart will answer, "Father, I never knew it, but it is true —I am ever with You, and all You have is mine." God has given all He has to Christ, and God longs that Christ should have you and me entirely. To every hungry heart I say, "If you want to live to the glory of God, seek one thing: to claim and believe that the presence of Jesus can be with you every moment of your life."

I want to speak about the presence of Jesus as it is set before us in that blessed story of Christ's walking on the sea. Come, look with me at some points that are suggested to us.

First, think of *the presence of Christ lost*. You know the disciples loved Christ, clung to Him, and delighted in Him, even with all their failings. But what happened? The

Master went up to the mountain to pray and
sent them across the sea alone without Him.
When a storm arose they toiled, rowed, and la-
bored, but the wind was against them. They
made no progress and were in danger of perish-
ing. How their hearts said, "If only the Master
were here!" But His presence was gone. They
missed Him. Once before they had been in a
storm, and Christ had said, *"Peace, be still"*
(Mark 4:39), and all was well. But here they
were in darkness, danger, and terrible trouble,
and no Christ to help them. Isn't that the life
of many believers at times? I get into darkness.
I have committed sin. The cloud is over me. I
miss the face of Jesus. For days I work, worry,
and labor, but it is all in vain. I miss the presence of Christ. Beloved, let us write that down:
**the presence Jesus lost is the cause of all
our wretchedness and failure**.

Look at the second step, the presence of
Jesus *dreaded*. They were longing for the
presence of Christ, and Christ came to them
after midnight. He came walking on the water
amid the waves, but they didn't recognize Him.
They cried out in fear, *"It is a spirit!"* (Matthew 14:26). Their beloved Lord was coming
near, and they knew Him not. They dreaded
His approach. How often have I seen a believer
dreading the approach of Christ—crying out

for Him, longing for Him, and yet dreading His coming. Why? Because Christ was coming in a fashion that they did not expect.

Perhaps some have been saying, "Alas! I fear I never can have the abiding presence of Christ." You have heard what we have said about a life in the Spirit, and about abiding always in the presence of God and in His fellowship, yet you have been afraid of it. You have said, "It is too lofty and too difficult." You have dreaded the very teaching that was going to help you. Jesus came to you in the teaching, but you didn't recognize Him.

Or, perhaps, He came in a way that you dreaded His presence. Perhaps God has been speaking to you about some sin. There is that sin of temper, of unlovingness, of unforgiveness, of worldliness and compromising fellowship with the world, that love of man and man's honor, that fear of man and man's opinion, or that pride and self-confidence. God has been speaking to you, yet you have been frightened. That was Jesus wanting to draw you close, but you were afraid. You don't see how you can give up all that. You are not ready to say, "At any sacrifice, I am going to have that taken out of me, and I will give it up." While Christ was approaching to bless you, you were afraid of Him.

Perhaps at other times, Christ has come to you with affliction. You have said, "If I want to be entirely holy, I know I will have to be afflicted, but I am afraid of affliction." You have dreaded the thought, "Christ may come to me in affliction." The presence of Christ dreaded! Oh, beloved, I want to tell you it is all misconception. The disciples had no reason to dread that "spirit" coming there, for it was Christ Himself. When God's Word comes close and touches your heart, remember that it is Christ out of whose mouth goes the two-edged sword, Christ in His love comes to cut away the sin, that He may fill your heart with God's love. Beware of dreading the presence of Christ.

Then comes the third thought: the presence of Christ *revealed*. Bless God! When Christ heard how they cried, he spoke the words of the text, *"Be of good cheer; it is I; be not afraid."* What joy those words brought to their hearts! There is Jesus. That dark object appears, that dreaded form. It is our blessed Lord Himself.

Friends, the Master's objective, whether it is by affliction or otherwise, is to prepare us for receiving the presence of Christ. Through it all Jesus speaks, *"It is I; be not afraid."* The presence of Christ revealed! I want to tell you that the Son of God is longing to reveal Himself to you. Listen! Is there any longing heart? Jesus says to you, *"Be of good cheer; it is I; be not afraid."*

Beloved, God has given us Christ. Does God want me to have Christ every moment? Without doubt. God wants the presence of Christ to be the joy of every hour of my life. If there is one thing sure, Christ can reveal Himself to me every moment. Are you willing to come and claim this privilege? He can reveal Himself. I cannot reveal Him to you; you cannot grasp Him; but He can shine into your heart. How can I see the sunlight tomorrow morning? The sunlight will reveal itself. How can I know Christ? Christ can reveal Himself.

Set your heart upon this, and offer this humble prayer, "Lord, reveal Yourself to me now, so that I may never lose sight of You. Give me to understand that through the thick darkness You come to make Yourself known." Let not one heart doubt, however dark it may be. At midnight—whatever midnight there be in the soul—in the dark, at midnight, Christ can reveal Himself. Thank God, often after a life of ten or twenty years of dawn, after a life of ten or twenty years of struggling, now in the light and now in the dark, Jesus is willing just to give Himself to us, never more to part. God grant us that presence of Jesus!

The presence of Jesus *desired* is the fourth thought. What happened? Peter heard the Lord, and he was content. He was in the boat. Some 30, 40, 50 yards away was Jesus, who acted as though He would have passed them. Peter, bless the Lord, Peter's heart was right with Christ, and he wanted to claim His presence. He said, *"Lord, if it be Thou, bid me come unto Thee on the water"* (Matthew 14:28).

Yes, Peter could not rest. He wanted to be as near to Christ as possible. He saw Christ walking on the water and remembered how Christ had said, *"Follow Me"* (Matthew 4:19). He remembered how Christ, with the miraculous draught of fishes, had proved that He was Master of the sea and the waters. Peter also remembered how Christ had stilled the storm. Without argument or reflection, all at once he said, "My Lord is manifesting Himself in a new way. There is my Lord exercising a new supernatural power. I can go to my Lord. He is able to make me walk where He walks." He wanted to walk like Christ and near Christ. He didn't say, "Lord, let me walk around the sea here," but rather, "Lord, let me come to You."

Friends, wouldn't you like to have the presence of Christ in this way? Not that Christ should come down to a worldly level, which is what many Christians would like. They want to continue their sinful, worldly walk; they want to continue in their old life; and they want Christ to come to them with His comfort, His presence, and His love. However, that cannot be. If I am to have the presence of Christ, I must walk as He walked. His walk was a supernatural one. He walked in the love and in the power of God.

Most people walk according to the circumstances in which they are. Most say, "I am depending upon circumstances for my religion." Hundreds of times, you hear people say, "My circumstances prevent my enjoying unbroken fellowship with Jesus." What were the circumstances that were around Christ? The wind and the waves—and Christ walked triumphant over circumstances. Peter said, "Like my Lord I can triumph over all circumstances. Anything around me is nothing if I have Jesus." He longed for the presence of Christ. May God work in us that, as we look at the life of Christ upon earth, as we look how Christ walked and conquered the waves, every one of us could say, "I want to walk like Jesus." If that is your heart's desire, you can expect the presence of Jesus. But as long as you want to walk on a lower level than Christ, as long as you want to have a little of the world and of self-will, do not expect to have the presence of Christ.

Near Christ and like Christ—the two things go together. Have you understood that? Peter wanted to walk like Christ so that he might get near Christ. It is this I want to offer every one of you. I say to the weakest believer, "With God's aid you can have the presence and fellowship of Christ all day long, your whole life through." I want to bring you that promise, but I must give God's condition: **walk like Christ, and you will always abide near Christ**. The presence of Christ invites you to come and have unbroken fellowship with Him.

We have just had the presence of Christ desired, and my next thought is this: the presence of Christ *trusted*. The Lord Jesus said, *"Come"* (Matthew 14:29), and what did Peter do? He stepped out of the boat. How did he dare to do it against all the laws of nature? He sought Christ; he heard Christ's voice; he trusted Christ's presence and power; and in the faith of Christ he said, "I can walk on the water," and stepped out of the boat. Here is Peter's turning point, his crisis.

Peter saw Christ in the manifestation of a supernatural power. Peter believed that supernatural power could work in himself and that he could live supernatural life. He believed this applied to walking on the sea. Here lies the whole secret of the life of faith. While

on this earth, Christ had supernatural power—
the power of heaven, the power of holiness, the
power of fellowship with God—and Christ can
give me grace to live as He lived. Like Peter, if
I will but look at Christ and say to Him, "Lord,
speak the word, and I will come," and if I will
listen to Christ saying, *"Come,"* I also will have
power to walk on the waves.

Have you ever seen a more beautiful or
more instructive symbol of the Christian life?
When I once preached on it many years ago,
the thought that filled my heart was this: the
Christian life can be compared to Peter walking on the waves—nothing so difficult and impossible without Christ, nothing so blessed and
safe with Christ. That is the Christian life—
impossible without Christ's nearness—but
most safe and blessed, however difficult, if I
only have the presence of Christ.

Believers, I have tried in these pages to
call you to a better life, to a spiritual life, to a
holy life, a life in the Spirit, to a life in fellowship with God. Only one thing can enable you
to live it: you must have the Lord Jesus hold
your hand every minute of the day. "But can
that be?" you ask. Yes, it can. "I have so much
to think of. Sometimes for four or five hours of
the day, I have to go into the very thick of
business and have some ten men standing

around me, each claiming my attention. How can I always have the presence of Jesus in these circumstances?" Beloved, because Jesus is your God and loves you wonderfully, He is able to make His presence more clear to you than that of ten men who are standing around you. If you will in every morning take time and enter into your covenant with Him, "Lord Jesus, nothing can satisfy me but Your abiding presence," He will give it to you. Peter trusted the presence of Christ and said, "If Christ calls me, I can walk on the waves to Him." Shall we also trust the presence of Christ?

To walk through all the circumstances and temptations of life is exactly like walking on the water: you have no solid ground under your feet. You do not know how strong the temptations of Satan may come. But do believe God wants you to walk in a supernatural life beyond human power. God wants you to live life in Christ Jesus. Do you want that life? Then, come and say, "Jesus, I have heard Your promise that Your presence will go with me. You have said, *'My presence shall go with thee'* (Exodus 33:14). Lord, I claim it. I trust You."

Now, the sixth step in this wonderful history is the presence of Christ *forgotten*. Peter got out of the boat and began to walk toward the Lord Jesus with his eyes fixed on Him. He trusted the presence of Christ and walked boldly over the waves. But all at once, he took his eyes off Jesus and began immediately to sink. There was Peter, his walk of faith at an end, all drenched, drowning, and crying, "Lord, help me!" There are some of you saying in your hearts, "Ah, that's what will become of your higher-life Christians." There are people who say, "You never can live that life. Do not talk of it. You will always be failing." Peter always failed before Pentecost. It was because the Holy Spirit had not yet come. Therefore, his experience teaches us that, while Peter was still in the life of the flesh, he had to fail somehow or another. But, thank God, there was One to lift him out of the failure. Our last point will be to prove that out of that failure he came into closer union with and deeper dependence on Jesus than ever before. But, first, listen while I speak to you about this failure.

Someone may say, "I have been trying to say, 'Lord, I will live it.' But, tell me, suppose failure comes, what then?" Learn from Peter what you ought to do. What did Peter do? The very opposite of what most of us do. What did he do when he began to sink? That very moment, without one word of self-reproach or self-condemnation, he cried, "Lord, help me!" I wish I could teach every Christian that.

I remember the time in my spiritual life when that became clear to me. Up to that time, when I failed, my only thought was to reproach and condemn myself, which I thought would do me good. However, I found it didn't. I learned from Peter that, the moment I fail, my task is to say, "Jesus, Master, help me!" The very moment I say that, Jesus does help me.

Remember, failure is not an impossibility. I can conceive of more than one Christian who said, "Lord, I claim the fullness of the Holy Ghost. I want to live every hour of every day filled with the Holy Spirit." I can also conceive of an honest soul who said that with trembling faith, yet may have fallen. I want to say to that one, "Don't be discouraged. If failure comes, at once, without waiting, appeal to Jesus. He is always ready to hear. The very moment you find there is the temper, the hasty word, or some other wrong, at once the living Jesus is near, so gracious and so mighty. Appeal to Him, and there will be help at once. If you will learn to do this, Jesus will lift you up and lead you on to a walk where His strength secures you from failure."

The presence of Jesus was forgotten while Peter looked at the waves, but, finally, we have the presence of Jesus *restored*. Yes, Christ stretched out His hand to save him. Possibly—

for Peter was a very proud, self-confident man—possibly he had to sink to teach him that his faith could not save him, but it was the power of Christ. God wants us to learn the lesson that when we fall, we can cry to Jesus, and at once He reaches out His hand. Remember, Peter walked back to the boat without sinking again. Why? Because Christ was very near him.

It is quite possible, if you use your failure rightly, to be far nearer Christ after it than before. That is, come and acknowledge, "In me there is nothing, but I am going to trust my Lord totally." Let every failure teach you to cling to Christ afresh, and He will prove Himself a mighty, loving Helper.

The presence of Jesus restored! Christ took Peter by the hand and helped him. I don't know whether they walked hand in hand those forty or fifty yards back to the boat, or whether Christ allowed Peter to walk·beside Him. However, I do know they were very near to each other, and it was the nearness to his Lord that strengthened him.

Remember what has taken place since that happened with Peter. The cross has been erected, the blood has been shed, the grave has been opened, the resurrection has been accomplished, heaven has been opened, and the Spirit of the Exalted One has come down. Do believe it is possible for the presence of Jesus to be with us every day, all the time. God has given you to Christ, and He wants to give Christ into your heart in such a way that His presence will be with you every moment of your life.

Who is willing to lift up his eyes and his heart and exclaim, "I want to live according to God's standard?" Who is willing? Who is willing to cast himself into the arms of Jesus and to live a life of faith, victorious over the winds and the waves, over the circumstances and difficulties? Who is willing to say, "Lord, bid me come to You upon the water"? Are you willing? Listen! Jesus says, *"Come."* Will you step out at this moment?

Over there is the boat, the old life that Peter had been leading. He had been familiar with the sea from his boyhood, and that boat was a very sacred place to him. Christ had sat beside him there. Christ had preached from that boat of Peter's. Christ had given the wonderful catch of fish into that boat. Thus, it was a very sacred boat. But Peter left it to come to a place more sacred still—walking with Jesus on the water—a new and a divine experience.

Your Christian life may be a very sacred thing. You may say, "Christ saved me by His blood. He has given me many experiences of

grace. God has proved His grace in my heart,"
but you confess, "I haven't got the real life of
abiding fellowship. The winds and the waves
often terrify me, and I sink." Come out of the
boat of past experiences at once. Come out of
the boat of external circumstances. Come out
of the boat, step out on the word of Christ, and
believe, "With Jesus I can walk on the water."

When Peter was in the boat, what did he
have between him and the bottom of the sea?
A couple of planks. But when he stepped out
on the water, what did he have between him
and the sea? Not a plank, but the word of Almighty Jesus. Will you come, and, without any
prior experience, rest on the word of Jesus,
*"Lo, I am with you always"*? Trust in His word,
*"Be of good cheer; it is I; be not afraid."*

Every moment Jesus lives in heaven.
Every moment by His Spirit, Jesus whispers
that word. Every moment He lives to make it
true. Accept it now! The Lord Jesus is equal to
every emergency and can meet the wants of
every soul. May our whole hearts say, "He can
and will do it!" Come, believers, let us claim it
most deliberately, most quietly, most rest-
fully—let us claim it.

# 7

## A Word to Workers

*Ye shall receive power after that the Holy Ghost
is come upon you, and ye shall be
witnesses unto Me.
—Acts 1:8*

S ome time ago I read this expression by
an old author: "The first duty of a clergyman is humbly to ask of God that all
that he wants done in his hearers should first
be truly and fully done in himself." These
words have stuck with me ever since. What a
solemn application this is to the subject that
has occupied our attention in previous chapters—the living and working in the fullness of
the Holy Spirit! Yet, if we understand our call-
ing correctly, every one of us will have to say,
"That is the one thing on which everything

depends." What profit is it to tell men that they may be filled with the Spirit of God, if, when they ask us, "Has God done it for you?" we have to answer, "No, He has not done it for me yet." What profit is it for me to tell men that Jesus Christ can dwell within us every moment, keeping us from sin and actual transgression, and the abiding presence of God can be our portion all day, if I do not wait upon God first to do it truly and fully daily in me?

Look at the Lord Jesus Christ. It was of Christ Himself, when He had received the Holy Ghost from heaven, that John the Baptist said, *"He shall baptize you with the Holy Ghost"* (Mark 1:8). I can only communicate to others what God has imparted to me. If my life as a minister is a life in which the flesh still greatly prevails and in which I grieve the Holy Spirit, I cannot expect anything but that my people will receive through me a very mingled kind of life. But if the life of God dwells in me and I am filled with His power, then I can hope that the life that goes out from me may be infused into my hearers also.

We have referred to the need of every believer to be filled with the Spirit. What is there of deeper interest to us now, or that can better occupy our attention, than prayerfully to consider how we can bring our congregations to believe that this is possible, and how we can lead every believer to seek it for himself, to expect it, and to accept it, so as to live it? But, the message must come from us as a witness of our personal experience by God's grace.

The same writer to whom I alluded, says elsewhere: "The first business of a clergyman, when he sees men awakened and brought to Christ, is to lead them on to know the Holy Spirit." How true! Don't we find this throughout the word of God? John the Baptist preached Christ as the *"Lamb of God which taketh away the sin of the world."* (John 1:29). We read in Matthew 3:11 that he also said that Christ would *"baptize you with the Holy Ghost and with fire."* In John 1:33, we read that the Baptist was told, *"Upon whom thou shalt see the Spirit descending, and remaining on Him, the same is He which baptizeth with the Holy Ghost."* Thus John the Baptist led the people on from Christ to the expectation of the Holy Ghost for themselves.

And what did Jesus do? For three years, He was with His disciples, teaching and instructing them. But when He was about to go away, in His farewell sermon on the last night, what was His great promise to the disciples? *"I shall pray the Father, and He shall give you another Comforter...even the Spirit of truth"*

(John 14:16-17). He had previously promised to those who believed on Him, that *"rivers of living water"* would flow from them, which John explained as meaning the Holy Ghost: *"This spake He of the Spirit"* (John 7:39).

But this promise was only to be fulfilled after Christ was glorified (see John 7:39). Christ points to the Holy Spirit as the one fruit of being glorified. **The glorified Christ leads to the Holy Ghost.** So in His farewell, Christ leads the disciples to expect the Spirit as the Father's great blessing. Then again, when Christ came and stood at the footstool of His heavenly throne, on the Mount of Olives, ready to ascend, what were His words? *"Ye shall receive power after that the Holy Ghost is come upon you, and ye shall be witnesses unto Me"* (Acts 1:8). Christ's constant work was to teach His disciples to expect the Holy Spirit.

As you look through the Book of Acts, you see the same thing. On the day of Pentecost, Peter preached that Christ was exalted and had received of the Father the promise of the Holy Ghost. So he told the people; *"Repent and be baptized...in the name of Jesus Christ for the remission of sins, and ye shall receive the gift of the Holy Ghost"* (Acts 2:38). So, when I believe in Jesus risen, ascended, and glorified, I will receive the Holy Ghost.

After Philip had preached the Gospel in Samaria, men and women had been converted, and there was great joy in the city. The Holy Spirit had been working, but something was still lacking. Peter and John came down from Jerusalem, prayed for the converted ones, *"laid their hands on them, and they received the Holy Ghost"* (Acts 8:17). Then they had the conscious possession and enjoyment of the Spirit. However, until that came, they were incomplete.

Paul was converted by the mighty power of Jesus, who appeared to him on the way to Damascus; yet he had to go to Ananias to receive the Holy Ghost. We also read that when Peter went to talk to Cornelius, as he preached Christ, *"the Holy Ghost fell on all them which heard the word"* (Acts 10:44). This Peter took as the sign that the Gentiles were one with the Jews in God's favor, having the same baptism.

And so we might go through many of the Epistles, where we find the same truth taught, Look at that wonderful epistle to the Romans. The doctrine of justification by faith is established in the first five chapters. In the sixth and seventh, though the believer is represented as dead to sin and the law, and married to Christ, yet a dreadful struggle goes on in the heart of the regenerate man as long as he does

not have the full power of the Holy Spirit. But
in the eighth chapter, it is the *"law of the
Spirit of life in Christ Jesus"* that makes us
free from *"the law of sin and death"* (v. 2). We
are *"not in the flesh, but in the Spirit"* (v. 9),
with the Spirit of God dwelling in us. All the
teaching leads us to the Holy Spirit.

Look at Galatians. We always talk of this
epistle as the great source of instruction on the
doctrine of justification by faith. But have you
ever noticed how the doctrine of the Holy
Spirit holds a most prominent place there?
Paul asks the Galatians: *"Received ye the Spirit
by the works of the law, or by the hearing of
faith?"* (v. 3:2). It was the hearing of faith that
led them to the fullness of the Spirit's power.
If they sought to be justified by the works of
the law, they had *"fallen from grace. For we
through Spirit wait for the hope of righteous-
ness by faith"* (vv. 5:4-5). And then at the end
of the fifth chapter, we are told, *"If we live in
the Spirit, let us walk in the Spirit"* (v. 25).

Again, if we go to the Corinthian epistles,
we find Paul asking the Christians in Corinth:
*"Know ye not that your body is the temple of the
Holy Ghost which is in you?"* (1 Corinthians
6:19). If we look into Ephesians, we find the
doctrine of Holy Spirit mentioned twelve
times. It is the Spirit that seals God's people;

*"Ye were sealed with that Holy Spirit of promise"* (v. 1:13). He illumines them, *"That God may give unto you the Spirit of wisdom and revelation in the knowledge of Him"* (v. 1:17). Through Christ, Jew and Gentile *"have access by one Spirit unto the Father"* (v. 2:18). They *"are builded together for an habitation of God through the Spirit"* (v. 2:22). They are *"strengthened with might by His Spirit in the inner man"* (v. 3:16). *"With all lowliness and meekness, with long-suffering, forbearing one another in love,* [they are] *endeavoring to keep the unity of the Spirit in the bond of peace"* (vv. 4:2-3), *"grieve not the Holy Spirit of God, whereby ye are sealed unto the day of redemption"* (v. 4:30). Being *"filled with the Spirit,"* we *"sing and make melody in our hearts to the Lord"* (v. 5:18), and thus glorify Him. Study these epistles carefully, and you will find that what I say is true—that Paul takes great pains to lead Christians to the Holy Spirit as the consummation of the Christian life.

It was the Holy Ghost who was given to the church at Pentecost. It is the Holy Ghost who gives Pentecostal blessings now. It is this power, given to bless men, that wrought such wonderful life, love, and self-sacrifice in the early church. It is this that makes us look back to those days as the most beautiful part of the

church's history. And it is the same Spirit of
power that must dwell in the hearts of all believers in our day to give the church its true
position. Let us ask God then, that every minister and Christian laborer may be endued
with the power of the Holy Ghost; that He may
search us and try us, and enable us sincerely to
answer the question, "Have I known the indwelling and the filling of the Holy Spirit that
God wants me to have?" Let each one of us ask
himself, "Is it my great study to know the Holy
Ghost dwelling in me, so that I may help others to yield to the same indwelling of the Holy
Spirit, and that He may reveal Christ fully in
His divine saving and keeping power?" Will not
every one have to confess, "Lord, I have all too
little understood this; I have all too little mani-
fested this in my work and preaching"?

Beloved, "The first duty of every clergyman is to humbly ask God that all that wants
done in his hearers may be first fully and truly
done in himself." "And the second thing is his
duty towards those who are awakened and
brought to Christ, to lead them on to the full
knowledge of the presence and indwelling of
the Holy Spirit." Now, if we are indeed to come
into full harmony with these two great princi-
ples then there comes to us some further
questions of the very deepest importance. The

first question is: "Why is it that there is in the church of Christ so little practical acknowledgment of the power of the Holy Ghost?" I am not speaking to you as if I thought you were not sound in doctrine on this point. I speak to you as believing in the Holy Ghost as the third person in the ever-blessed Trinity. But I speak to you confidently as to those who will readily admit that the truth of the presence and power of the Holy Ghost is not acknowledged in the church as it ought to be. The question is, Why not? I think the answer is because of its spirituality. It is one of the most difficult truths in the Bible for the human mind to comprehend. God has revealed Himself in creation throughout the universe. He has revealed Himself in Christ incarnate—and what a subject of study the person, word, and works of Christ form! But the mysterious indwelling of the Holy Spirit, hidden in the depths of the life of the believer, is so much less easy to comprehend!

In the early Pentecostal days of the church, this knowledge was intuitive. They possessed the Spirit in power. But soon after the spirit of the world began to creep into the church and mastered it. This was followed by the deeper darkness of formality and superstition in the Roman Catholic Church, when the spirit of the world completely triumphed in what was improperly styled the church of Christ. The Reformation in the days of Luther restored the truth of justification by faith in Christ. However, the doctrine of the Holy Ghost did not obtain its proper place then, for God does not reveal all truth at one time. Thus, much of the worldly spirit was still left in the reformed churches. Now God is awakening the church to strive after a fuller idea of the Holy Spirit's place and power. Through books, discussions, and conventions many hearts are being stirred.

Beloved, it is our privilege to take part in this great movement. Let us engage in it more earnestly than ever. Let each of us say, My great work is to lead men to the acknowledging of the Holy Spirit, who alone can glorify Christ. I may try to glorify Christ in my efforts, but it will avail nothing without the Spirit of God. I may urge men to practice holiness and every Christian virtue, but all my persuasion will avail very little unless I help them to believe that they must have the Holy Ghost dwelling in them every moment to enable them to live the life of Christ.

The great reason why the Holy Spirit was given from heaven was to make Christ's presence manifest to us. While Jesus was incarnate, His disciples were too much under the power of the flesh to allow Him to lodge in their hearts. It was necessary, He said, that He should go away, in order that the Spirit might come. To those who loved Him and kept His commandments, He promised that He and the Father would also come with the Spirit and make Their abode with them. Thus, the Holy Spirit's great work is to reveal the Father and the Son in the hearts of God's people. If we believe and teach men that the Holy Spirit can make Christ a reality to them, men will learn to believe and accept Christ's presence and power, of which they now know far too little.

Then another question presents itself, namely, What are we to expect when the Holy Spirit is duly acknowledged ant received? I ask this question, because I have frequently noticed something with considerable interest and with some anxiety. I sometimes hear men praying earnestly for a baptism of the Holy Spirit so that He may give them power for their work. Beloved, we need this power, not only for work, but for our daily lives. Remember, we must have it all the time.

In Old Testament times, the Spirit came with power upon the prophets and other inspired men, but He did not dwell permanently in them. Similarly, the Holy Spirit came with power to work miraculous gifts in the Corinthian church, yet they had but a small measure of His sanctifying grace. You will remember the carnal strife, envying, and divisions. They had gifts of utterance, knowledge, and wisdom, etc.; but pride, unlovingness, and other sins sadly marred the character of many of them.

What does this teach us? That a **man may have a great gift of power for work, but very little of the indwelling Spirit**. In 1 Corinthians 13, we are reminded that though we may have faith that would remove mountains, if we have not love, we are nothing. We must have the love that brings the humility and self-sacrifice of Jesus. Don't give priority to the gifts we may possess. If we do, we will have very little blessing. But we should seek, first, that the Spirit comes as a light and power of holiness from the indwelling Jesus. Let the first work of the Holy Spirit be to humble you deep down, so that your whole life will be a tender, broken-hearted waiting on God in the consciousness of mercy coming from above.

Do not seek large gifts. You need something deeper. It is not enough that a tree shoots its branches to the sky and is covered thickly with leaves. We want its roots to strike deeply into the soil also. Let the thought of the Holy Spirit's being in us, and our hope of being filled with the Spirit, always be accompanied with a broken and contrite heart in us. Let us bow low before God, in waiting for His grace to fill and sanctify us. We do not want power that God might allow us to use, while our inner part is unsanctified. We want God to give us full possession of Himself. In due time, the special gift may come, but we want first the power of the Holy Ghost working something far mightier and more effectual in us than any such gift. Therefore, seek not only a baptism of power, but a baptism of holiness. Seek that the inner nature be sanctified by the indwelling of Jesus. Then other power will come as needed.

A third point of discussion now arises. Suppose some one says to me: "I have given myself up to be filled with the Spirit, and I do not feel that there is any difference in my condition. I can speak of no change of experience. What must I think? Was my surrender not honest?" No, do not think that. "But what then? Does God give no response?" Beloved, God gives a response, but that is not always within certain months or years.

"What, then, would you have me do?" Retain the position you have taken before God, and maintain it every day. Say, "Oh, God, I have given myself to be filled. Here I am an empty vessel, trusting and expecting to be filled by You." Take that position every day, every hour. Ask God to write it across your heart. Give up to God an empty, consecrated vessel that He may fill it with His Spirit. Take that position constantly. It may be that you are not fully prepared. Ask God to cleanse you and to give you grace to separate from everything sinful—from unbelief or whatever hindrance there may be. Then take your position before God and say, "My God, You are faithful. I have entered into covenant with You for Your Spirit to fill me, and I believe You will fulfill it." I say for myself and for every Christian worker, man or woman, that if we thus come before God with a full surrender, with a bold, believing attitude, God's promise must be fulfilled.

If you were to ask me of my own experience, I would say this: There have been times when I hardly knew what to think of God's answer to my prayer in this matter. But I have found it my joy and my strength to take and maintain position, and say: "My God, I have given myself to You. It was Your grace that led me to Christ. I stand before You in confidence that You will keep Your covenant with me to the end. I am the empty vessel. You are the God that fills all." **God is faithful, and He gives the promised blessing in His own time and method**. Beloved, for God's sake, be content with nothing less than full health and spiritual life. *"Be filled with the Spirit."*

Let me return now to the two expressions with which I began: "The first duty of every clergyman is humbly to ask of God that all that he wants done in those who hear his preaching may be first truly and fully done in himself." Beloved, I ask you, is it not the longing of your hearts to have a congregation of believers filled with the Holy Ghost? Is it not your unceasing prayer for the church of Christ, that the Spirit of holiness, the very Spirit of God's Son, the spirit of unworldliness and of heavenly-mindedness, may possess the church; and that the Spirit of victory and of power over sin may fill its children? If you are willing for that to come, your first duty is to have it yourself.

And then the second statement: "The first duty of every clergyman is to lead those who have been brought to Christ to be entirely filled with the Holy Ghost." How can I do my work with success? I can conceive what a privilege it is to be led by the Spirit of God in all that I am doing. In studying my Bible, praying, visiting, organizing, or whatever I am doing, God is willing to guide me by His Holy Spirit. It sometimes becomes a humiliating experience for me that I am unwatchful and do not wait for the blessing. When that is the case, God can bring me back again.

But there is also the blessed experience of God's guiding hand, often through deep darkness, by His Holy Spirit. Let's walk about among the people as men of God, that we may not only talk about a book and what we believe with our hearts to be true, but may tell what we are and have in our own experience.

Jesus calls us **witnesses** for Him. What does that mean? The Holy Ghost brought down from heaven to men a participation in the joy and glory of the exalted Christ. Peter and the others who spoke with Him were filled with this heavenly Spirit. Thus Christ spoke through them and accomplished the work for them.

Beloved, if you and I are Christ's, we should take our places and claim our privilege. We are witnesses to the truth which we believe—witnesses to the reality of what Jesus does and what He is, by His presence in our own souls. If we are willing to be such witnesses for Christ, let us go to our God. Let us make confession and surrender, and by faith claim what God has for us as workers in His service. God will prove faithful. Even at this moment, He will touch our hearts with a deep consciousness of His faithfulness and presence and will give to every hungering, trustful one that which we continually need.

# 8

# *Consecration*

*But who am I, and what is my people, that we
should be able to offer so willingly after this
sort? for all things come of Thee, and
of Thine own have we given Thee.*
—*1 Chronicles 29:14*

To be able to offer anything to God is a
perfect mystery. Consecration is a miracle of grace. *"All things come of Thee,
and of Thine own have we given Thee."* In
these words are four very precious thoughts I
want to try to make clear to you:

1. God is the Owner of all, and gives all to us.
2. We have nothing but what we receive, but
   everything we need we may receive from
   God.

3. It is our privilege and honor to give back to God what we receive from Him.
4. God has a double joy in His possessions when He receives back from us what He gave.

When I apply this to my life—to my body, to my wealth, to my property, to my whole being with all its powers—then I understand what consecration ought to be.

**The glory and nature of God is to be always giving**. God is the Owner of all. There is no power, no riches, no goodness, no love outside of God. It is the very nature of God that He does not live for Himself, but for His creatures. His is a love that always delights to give. Here we come to the first step in consecration. I must see that everything I have is given by Him. I must learn to believe in God as the great Owner and Giver of all. I have nothing but what actually and definitely belongs to God. Just as much as people mistakenly say, "This money in my purse belongs to me," so God is truly the Proprietor of all. It is His only. It is His life and delight to be always giving.

Grasp this precious thought: **There is nothing that God has that He does not want to give**. It is His nature. Therefore, when God asks anything of you, He must give it first Himself, and He will. Never be afraid whatever God asks, for God only asks what is His own. What He asks you to give, He will first give to you. The Possessor, Owner, and Giver of all is our God. You can apply this to yourself, your powers, and to all you are and have. Study it, believe it, live in it every day, every hour, every moment.

Just as the nature and glory of God is to be always giving, **the nature and glory of man is to be always receiving**. What did God make us for? Each of us have been made to be a vessel into which God can pour His life, His beauty, His happiness, His love. Every one is created to be a receptacle and a reservoir of divine heavenly life and blessing.

Have we understood that our great work—the object of our creation—is to be always receiving? If we fully enter into this, it will teach some precious things. One thing is the utter folly of being proud or conceited. What an idea! If I were to borrow a very beautiful coat and walk about boasting of it as if it were my own, you might say, "What a fool!" The Everlasting God owns everything we have, yet will we dare to exalt ourselves on account of what is all His? What a blessed lesson it will teach us about what our position is! God's nature is to be always giving, and mine to be always receiving. Just as the lock and key fit each other, God the

Giver and I the receiver fit into each other. How often we worry about things and about praying for them, instead of going back to the root and saying, "Lord, I only crave to be the receptacle of what the will of God means for me—of the power, the gifts, the love, and the Spirit of God." What can be simpler?

Come as a receptacle—cleansed, emptied and humble. Come, and then God will delight to give. With reverence I say, He cannot help Himself. It is His promise, His nature. The blessing is ever flowing out of Him. You know how water always flows into the lowest places. If we would but be emptied and lowly, nothing but receptacles, what a blessed life we could live! Daily just praising Him—He gives and I accept. He bestows and I rejoice to receive.

Hundreds of thousands of people have said today, "What a beautiful morning! Let's open the windows and bring in the sunlight with its warmth and cheerfulness!" May our hearts learn every moment to drink in the light and sunshine of God's love. *"Who am I, and what is my people, that we should be able to offer so willingly after this sort? for all things come of Thee, and we have given Thee of Thine own."*

If God gives all and I receive all, then the third thought is very simple: **I must give all back again**. What a privilege that for the sake

of having me in loving, grateful relationship
with Him, and giving me the happiness of
pleasing and serving Him, God should say,
"Come now, and bring Me back all that I give."
Yet people say, "Oh, but must I give *everything*
back?" Beloved, don't you know that there is
no happiness or blessedness except in giving to
God? David felt it. He said, "Lord, what an
blessed privilege it is to be allowed to give back
to You that which is Yours!" Just to receive
and then to render back in love to Him what
He gives. Do you know what God needs you
for? People say, "Doesn't God give us all good
gifts to enjoy?" But do you know that **the reality of the enjoyment is in the giving back?**

Just look at Jesus. God gave Him a wonderful body. He kept it holy and gave it as a
sacrifice to God. This is the beauty of having a
body. God has given you a soul. This is the
beauty of having a soul—you can give it back
to God. People talk about the difficulty they
have with being so strong-willed. You never
can have too strong a will, but the trouble is
we do not give that strong will up to God to
make into a vessel in which He can pour His
Spirit, to fit it to do splendid service for Him.

We have now had the three thoughts: God
gives all; I receive all; I give up all. Will you do
this now? Will not every heart say, "My God,

teach me to give up everything"? Take your head, your mind with all its powers of thought, your tongue with all its power of speaking, your property, your heart with its affections— the best and most secret—your gold and silver, everything, lay it at God's feet, and say, "Lord, here is the covenant between You and me. You delight to give all, and I delight to give back all." God, teach us that. If that simple lesson were learned, there would be an end of so much trouble about finding out the will of God, and an end of all our holding back, for it would be written, not upon our foreheads, but across our hearts, "God can do with me what He pleases; I belong to Him with all I have." Instead of always saying to God "Give, give, give," we should say, "Yes, Lord, You do give, You do love to give, and I love to give back." Try that life and find out if it is not the very highest life.

God gives all. I receive all. I give all back. Now comes the final thought: **God rejoices in what we give to Him**. It is not only I that am the receiver and the giver, but God is the Giver and the Receiver too. I say with reverence, God has more pleasure in receiving back than even in giving. With our little faith, we often think they come back to God all defiled. God says, "No, they come back beautiful and glorified."

The surrender of the dear child of His, with his aspirations and thanksgiving, brings it to God with a new value and beauty. Child of God, **you do not know how precious the gift that you bring to your Father is in His sight**. Have I not seen a mother give a piece of cake, and the child comes and offers her a piece to share it with her? How she values the gift! My friends, your God, His heart, His Father's heart of love, longs, to have you give Him everything. It is a demand, but it is not a demand of a hard Master. It is the call of a loving Father, who knows that every gift you bring to Him will bind you closer to Himself, and every surrender you make will open your heart wider to receive more of His gifts. A gift to God has in His sight infinite value. It delights Him. He sees of the travail of His soul and is satisfied. And it brings unspeakable blessing to you.

These are the thoughts our text suggests; now comes the practical application. What are the lessons? We here learn what the true disposition of the Christian life is: **to be and abide in continual dependence upon God**. Become nothing. Begin to understand that you are nothing but an earthen vessel into which God will shine down the treasure of His love. Blessed is the man who knows what it is to be nothing, to be just an empty vessel meet for

God's use. "Work," Paul says, *"for it is God who worketh in you to will and to do"* (Philippians 2:13).

Beloved, come and take the place of deep dependence on God. Then take the place of childlike trust and expectancy. Count upon your God to do for you everything that you can desire of Him. Honor God as a God who gives liberally. Honor God and believe that He asks nothing from you but what He is going first to give. And then come praise and surrender in consecration. Praise Him for it! Let every sacrifice to Him be a thank-offering.

What are we going to consecrate? First of all, our lives. There are perhaps young men and women whose hearts are asking, "What do you want me to do—say I will be a missionary?" No, indeed, I do not ask you to do this. Deal with God. Come to Him and say, "Lord of all, I belong to You, I am absolutely at Your disposal." Yield up yourselves. There may be many who cannot go as missionaries, but can give up themselves to God just the same to be consecrated to His work. Let us bow down before Him and give Him all our powers—our heads to think for His kingdom, our hearts to go out in love for men. However feeble you may be, say: "Lord, here I am, to live and die for Your kingdom."

Some talk and pray about the filling of the Holy Spirit. Let them pray and believe more. But remember the Holy Spirit came to fit men to be messengers of the kingdom. You can't expect to be filled with the Spirit unless you want to live for Christ's kingdom. You can't expect the love, peace, and joy of heaven to come into your life and be your treasures unless you give them up absolutely to God, possessing and using them only for Him. **The soul utterly given up to God will receive in its emptying the fullness of the Holy Spirit**.

Friends, we must consecrate not only ourselves—body and soul—but all we have. Some of you may have children; perhaps you have an only child, and you dread the very idea of letting it go. Take care. God deserves your confidence, love, and surrender. I plead with you to take your children and say to Jesus: "Anything, Lord, that pleases You." Educate your children for Jesus. God help you to do it. He may not accept of all of them, but He will accept of the will, and there will be a rich blessing in your soul for it.

Then there is money. When I hear appeals for money from every ministry, when I hear calculations as to what the Christians of England are spending on pleasure and the small amount given for missions, I say something is terrible in it. God's children with so much wealth and comfort, giving away so small a portion! God be praised for every exception! Many give very little, never give so that it costs them something, and they feel it. Friends, our giving must be in proportion to God's giving. He gives you all. Let us take it up in our consecration prayer: "Lord, take it all, every penny I possess. It is all Yours." Let us often say, "It is all His." You may not know how much you ought to give. Give all, put everything in His hands, and He will teach you if you will wait.

We have heard this precious message from David's mouth. Present-day Christians, have we learned to know our God who is willing to give everything? May God help us to. Secondly, we have nothing that we do not receive, and we may receive everything if we are willing to receive from God. Thirdly, whatever you have received from God, give it back. It will bring a double blessing to your soul. Finally, whatever God receives back from us gives Him infinite joy and happiness, because He sees His object has been attained.

Let us come in the spirit of David, with the spirit of Christ in us. Let us pray our consecration prayer. May the Blessed Spirit give us grace to think and to say the right thing, and to do what is pleasing in the Father's sight.